DESHUMBERT'S
DICTIONARY OF DIFFICULTIES

met with in

Reading, Writing, Translating, and Speaking

FRENCH.

BY

MARIUS DESHUMBERT,

PROFESSOR OF FRENCH AT THE STAFF COLLEGE,
AND THE ROYAL MILITARY COLLEGE.

SIXTH EDITION.
(Fourth and Fifth Thousand.)

Copyright © 2013 Read Books Ltd.
This book is copyright and may not be
reproduced or copied in any way without
the express permission of the publisher in writing

British Library Cataloguing-in-Publication Data
A catalogue record for this book is available from the
British Library

PREFACE.

EVERY " *Professeur* " of French has met with translations similar to the following:—

a. " Il est *blessé*," " he is blessed " (instead of " he is wounded ").

b. " The dog's *hair*," " les *cheveux* du chien," which sounds just as droll to a Frenchman as " the dog's wig" would to an Englishman.

c. " La *veille* de Noël elle fut très malade," " *Old Mrs.* de Noël was very ill," in which the mistake *vieille* for *veille* was made readily enough.

d. " Je vous le *défends*," I *defend* you (for, I *forbid* you to do it). †

The above examples may be considered as *types* of four different kinds of mistakes, unfortunately very common, and for which grammars offer no remedy.

---

† I have even seen the sentences: " *Un épagneul de forte taille* " (a large spaniel) translated by: " A Spaniard with forty tails "; *un timbre poste*, by " a timber post "; *le pauvre enfant était un vrai magot*, by " the poor child was really a maggot "; *depuis cette époque les lions ont baissé de taille*, by " since that time lions have lowered their tails "; *il vit le doge*, by " he saw through the dodge "; *le nègre avait cinq pieds six pouces*, " the nigger used to have five feet and six thumbs "; *il lui jeta un coup d'œil*, " he gave him a blow on the eye." Speaking of a " snowy " forest, a French poet (JULES FORGET) said:— The translation handed to me was:—

Drapée en son manteau léger   Wrapped up in its light
Qui resplendit, la forêt semble   Shining cloak, the forest looks like
     Un grand verger.   A tall verger.

This little book will enable the students to avoid all such errors; it contains :—

1. Words belonging to the class mentioned in example *a*—that is, *French* words which *appear so English-like* as often to deceive learners, especially if the context somewhat favours the wrong translation (see " *Actuel,*" " *Courtier,*" " *Hisser* ").

2. English words belonging to type *b*.

If the reader has had occasion to speak to French people in their own language, he must have sometimes been unpleasantly surprised by a smile on his hearers' faces, warranted by nothing in the conversation. Of course, he perceived at once that he had inadvertently said something which sounded very funny to French ears. Again, although he, as he thought, spoke very clearly, he sometimes altogether failed to make himself understood. To avoid such vexation in future, let him study carefully those cases in which *different* meanings of the *same* English word are translated by *different* words in French (see " *Box,*" " *Case,*" " *Hand* ").

3. Words belonging to type *c*—that is, French words, such as *dénoûment* and *dénument*, which, although spelt and pronounced *nearly* alike, differ *widely* in their meanings.

4. A list of French words belonging to type *d*—that is, which have different meanings, and are translated by different English words (see " *Esprit* ").

5. Lastly, a list of those words which, although having the same meanings in both languages, differ somewhat in their respective spelling (see "*Language*"). These words have been added especially in view of the French dictation set at the Sandhurst and Woolwich Examinations.

This book contains also some practical observations and remarks not coming under any of the above heads, and not usually found in grammars (see "*Chaud*").

The gender of the French nouns is throughout shown by the article which precedes them.

All the words and remarks contained in this book are arranged in alphabetical order, so as to facilitate reference.

MARIUS DESHUMBERT.

Staff College,
    Camberley.

TO THE STUDENT.

You will probably spare yourself some mortification if—instead of waiting until you have *actually* made the mistakes pointed out in this book, and been *corrected* by the half-suppressed smile which you will be quick to detect on the faces of your listeners—you carefully read every page of this **Dictionary of Difficulties,** and mark with a pen or pencil the paragraphs which contain "something you did not know before."

At first, perhaps, you will not follow my advice, but will use this book as you do any other dictionary, that is to say, open it only *after* meeting with a difficulty; but would it not be wiser to make yourself familiar *beforehand* with these *danger-signals,* and thus avoid the pitfalls?

I, therefore, strongly advise the student to learn thoroughly a page, or half-a-page, every day. A task, however small it may be, if done daily and conscientiously will ensure success.

THE AUTHOR.

DESHUMBERT'S
DICTIONARY OF DIFFICULTIES

met with in

Reading, Writing, Translating, and Speaking

French.

N.B.—All French words throughout this book are in *italics* or followed by an asterisk (*).

A

Un **abattement***. . . . prostration, low spirits, despondency.
Tomber dans l'abattement, to become low spirited.

An **abatement**. . *une diminution;* (Business) *un rabais, une remise.*

Abbreviation . . (notice the spelling) *une abréviation.*

Notice the following abbreviations:—
7bre for **Septembre.**
8bre ,, **Octobre.**
9bre ,, **Novembre.**
10bre or Xbre ,, **Décembre.**

According to the old Roman Calendar, the year began in March; therefore September was (as its name implies) the seventh month, October the eighth, etc.

An **abundance**	(notice the spelling) *une ab**on**dance.* *Parler d'abondance,* to speak extempore. *Abondance de biens ne nuit pas,* Store is no sore. There cannot be too much of a good thing.
Abuser*	(*quelqu'un*) to deceive somebody. Ex.: *Je ne veux point vous abuser,* I do not wish to deceive you.
S'**Abuser***	to mistake one's self. Ex.: *Il vous a écrit, si je ne m'abuse,* he has written to me, if I am not mistaken.
Abuser de*	to impose upon, to make bad use of. Ex.: *Il abuse de votre bonté,* he takes advantage of your kindness.
To **abuse**	(to insult) *insulter, dire des sottises à, injurier* (see "*injurier*").
Un **accès***	(*a*) access, approach. (*b*) a fit (of anger, &c.).
Un **accomplissement*** **Accomplishment**	fulfilment. *talent* (or *art*) *d'agrément.*
Accorder*	(*a*) to grant (a request, &c.). (*b*) to tune (piano, &c.).
S'**accorder***	to agree (*see* " to agree ").
Achever* To **achieve**	to finish. *accomplir.*
Une **acre*** **Acre***	an acre. acrid.

An **act** . . .	(notice the spelling) *un act**e***. Taken in the act, *pris sur le fait*, or *pris en flagrant délit*.
Une **action*** . .	(*a*) an action. (*b*) a share (in railways, &c.). *Un actionnaire*, a shareholder.
Actuel* . . .	present (adjective). Ex.: *Les dangers actuels*, the present dangers.
Actual . . .	*réel, véritable*. Ex.: The actual amount, *la somme réelle*.
Actuellement* .	now, at this very moment. Ex.: *Il est malade actuellement*, he is ill now.
Actually . . .	*réellement, positivement, véritablement*. Ex.: He is actually ill, *il est réellement malade*.
To **add** . . .	(to make an addition) *additionner*. (to increase) *augmenter*. Ex.: He added to my misery, *il augmenta mon malheur*. (to join) *ajouter*. Ex.: You must add a piece to this material, *il faut ajouter un morceau à cette étoffe*.
An **address**. . .	(notice the spelling) *une ad**r**ess**e***.
Affermir* . .	to strengthen.
Affirmer* . .	to affirm.

Un **affidé***	a confederate, a secret agent.
Affilé*	sharp (sword, &c.).
Affilié*	affiliated (to an association, &c.).
Age	(time of life) *âge*. Ex.: At his age he ought to know better, *à son âge il devrait être plus raisonnable*.
	(century) *un siècle*.
	Old age, *la vieillesse*.
	The Middle Ages, *le moyen âge*.
	A middle-aged man, *un homme entre deux âges. Un homme d'une quarantaine* (or *d'une cinquantaine*) *d'années*.
	To be of age, *être majeur*.
	Under age, *mineur*.
Aggressive	(notice the spelling) *agressif*.
Agréer*	(*a*) to accept. Ex.: *Agréez mes remercîments*, accept my thanks.
	(*b*) to please. Ex.: *Venez, si cela vous agrée*, come, if it pleases you.
To **agree**	*s'accorder, s'entendre*. Ex.: They cannot agree, *ils ne peuvent s'accorder* or *s'entendre*.
Les **agréments***	the charms, the pleasures. Ex.: *Les agréments de la campagne*.
	Talents (or *arts*) *d'agrément*, accomplishments.
An **agreement**	*un accord, une convention*.
Un **aide***	a male assistant.
Une **aide***	(*a*) help, succour.
	(*b*) a female assistant.

Un **aigle***	(a) an eagle (the male).
	(b) a superior genius.
Une **aigle***	(a) an eagle (the female).
	(b) a military standard (of the Romans, &c.).

Une **aiguille***	a needle (pronounce ai-gu-i-ye).
Une **anguille***	an eel (pronounce an-ghi-ye).

Ailleurs*	elsewhere.
D'ailleurs*	besides, moreover.

Air (mas.)*	(a) air (atmosphere).
	(b) a tune.
	(c) look, appearance.
	Il a l'air bien portant, he looks well (in good health).
	Il a l'air malade, he looks ill.
Aire (fem.)*	(a) threshing-floor.
	(b) eyrie (nest of a bird of prey).

Alcohol	(notice the spelling) *alcool*.

Alléger*,	(a) to lighten, to unload (boats &c.).
	(b) to allay, to soothe (pain or grief).
Alléguer*	to allege.

Aller*	(a) to go. Ex.: *Il va à la campagne*, he goes down to the country.
	(b) to suit. Ex.: *Cela vous va-t-il?* Does that suit you? Do you agree to that?

DICTIONARY OF DIFFICULTIES.

Aller* *(continued)* . (c) to fit. Ex.: *Cet habit ne vous va pas*, this coat does not fit you.
(d) to match. Ex.: *Ces couleurs vont bien ensemble*, these colours match well.
(e) to be becoming. Ex.: *Le rose lui va très bien*, pink becomes her.
Allons donc, vous plaisantez, nonsense, you are joking.
Allons, restez tranquille, come, be quiet.
Comment allez-vous ? How do you do?
Il y va de la vie, life is at stake.
Il fait froid, allez ! It is cold, I assure you!

Allonger* . . . to lengthen.
Longer* . . . to go along, alongside. Ex.: *Nous longerons la rivière*, we shall walk (drive, ride, etc.) along the river.

Altéré* . . . (a) thirsty. Ex.: *Ce ragoût m'a altéré*, this stew has made me thirsty.
(b) altered (for the worse). Ex.: *Des traits altérés par la maladie*, features altered by sickness.

Altered . . . *changé*.

Une **amande*** . . an almond.
Une **amende*** . . a fine.
Mettre à l'amende or *condamner à une amende*, to fine.
Faire amende honorable, to apologize publicly.

Amiable	(notice the spelling) *ai*mable.
Une **ancre***	an anchor. *Jeter l'ancre*, to cast anchor. *Lever l'ancre*, to weigh anchor.
Encre (fem.)*	ink.
Anoblir*	to confer nobility on, to raise to the peerage.
Ennoblir*	to dignify, to ennoble.
Une **apologie***	a vindication, a justification.
Apologies	*des excuses.* To apologize, *s'excuser, faire des excuses.*
Un **appareil***	an apparatus.
An **apparel**	*un habit, un vêtement.*
Un **appartement***	a suite of rooms, a flat.
An **apartment**	*une chambre, une pièce* (see "*pièce*").
An **appearance**	(notice the spelling) *une appa-rence.*
To **appease**	(notice the spelling) *a*paiser.
Appointements (mas.)*	salary of a clerk.
An **appointment**	(to a post) *un emploi, une nomination.* (to meet somebody) *un rendez-vous.* Ex.: I have made an appointment with him for twelve o'clock, *je lui ai donné rendez-vous pour midi.*

Des **apprêts** (mas.)*	preparations.
Après*	after.
Apricot	(notice the spelling) un *abricot*.
Un **archer***.	a bowman, an archer.
Un **archet***	a violin bow.
Arçon (mas.)*	saddle-bow. *Vider les arçons*, to be unhorsed.
Arson	*un incendie dû à la malveillance*.
Aristocracy	(notice the spelling) *aristocra***tie** (pronounce aristocracie).
Un **artificier***	a firework maker.
An **artificer**	*un artisan, un ouvrier*.
Assailant	(notice the spelling) *un assai*ll*ant*.
Les **assistants***	by-standers, lookers-on, spectators.
Un **assistant***	an assistant, a help. An assistant in a shop *un commis de magasin*.
Assister*	(*quelqu'un*) to assist, to help somebody.
Assister à*	(*quelque chose*) to be present at, to attend. Ex.: *Il assistait à vos conférences*, he used to attend your lectures. *Il assista à la mort du roi*, he was present at the death of the King.
Un **associé***	a partner (*see* partner).
An **associate**	*un compagnon*.

Assommer*	(a) to beat to death. (b) to knock down (with a blow on the head). (c) to bore, to worry. Ex.: *Cet enfant m'assomme de ses questions*, this child worries me with his questions.
Un **atelier***	(a) a workshop. (b) a studio.
An **attempt**	(on somebody's life) *un attentat (contre la vie de quelqu'un)*. (an endeavour) *un essai, un effort*.
Attendre*	to wait.
S'**attendre à***	to expect. Ex.: *Je m'attendais à cette réponse*, I expected this answer. *Se faire attendre*, to keep people waiting. *Attendez-vous y!* I wish you may get it! (ironical).
To **attend**	(to listen) *faire attention, écouter*. (to be present at) *assister à*. (to accompany) *accompagner*. (a patient) *soigner (un malade)*. (to one's business) *vaquer (à ses affaires)*.
Attendrir*	(a) to make tender. (b) to excite pity *or* to move to pity.
Attirer*	to attract.
To **attire**	(to dress) *vêtir*. (to adorn) *parer, orner*.
Une **audience***	(a) an audience (of a sovereign). (b) a sitting (court of justice).
An **audience**	(an assembly) *un auditoire*.

An **authority**	(notice the spelling) *une autorité.* I have it on good authority, *je le tiens de bonne part* (or, *de bonne source*).
En **avance***	in advance. *Venir en avance,* to come before one's time *or* too soon.
En **avant***	forward, onward. *En avant de,* in front of.
Avertir*	to warn, to inform.
To **avert**	*détourner, écarter, empêcher.*
To **advertise**	*faire des annonces.*
Un **avertissement***	a warning.
An **advertisement**	*une annonce.*
Aveuglement (subst.)*	blindness (figuratively).
Aveuglément (adv.)*	blindly.
Aviser*	to inform, to apprise.
To **advise**	*conseiller.*
Un **axe***	an axis.
An **axe**	*une hache.*

B

Un **bac***	a ferry, a ferry-boat.
The **back**	(of persons and animals) *le dos.* (of a chair) *le dossier (d'une chaise).* (of a house) *le derrière (d'une maison).* (of the head) *le derrière (de la tête).*

The **back** (*continued*)	A hunchback, *un bossu*.
	To break any one's back, *casser les reins à quelqu'un*.
	To turn one's back on any one *tourner le dos à quelqu'un*.
Bagatelle (fem.)*	(*a*) bagatelle (a game).
	(*b*) a trifle, a bauble. Ex.: *Se fâcher pour une bagatelle*, to get angry about a trifle.
Baggage	(notice the spelling) *des bagages*.
Une **bague***	a ring (for the finger).
A **bag**	*un sac*.
Un **bail***	a lease (plural *des baux*).
A **bail**	*une caution, un cautionnement*. On bail, *sous caution*.
Se **baisser***	to stoop (see "to stoop").
S'**abaisser***	to humble one's self.
A **ball**	(in a general sense) *une boule*.
	(of a rifle) *une balle*.
	(of a cannon) *un boulet*.
	(at billiards) *une bille*.
	(of cotton) *un peloton*.
	(of india-rubber *or* leather filled with air) *un ballon*.
	(at tennis) *une paume*.
	(of the eye) *un globe*.
	(cup and ball) *un bilboquet*.
	(entertainment) *un bal* (plur. *des bals*).
	A fancy ball, *un bal costumé*.
Ballast	(railway line) *du balast*.
	(ship) *du lest*.

A **bandage**	(over the eyes) *un bandeau*. (over a wound) *un bandage*.
A **bank**	(commerce) *une banque*. (of a river) *une rive, un rivage*. Savings bank, *caisse d'épargne*.
Une **baraque*** The **barracks**	a hut, a hovel. *la caserne*.
Une **baratte*** Une **barrette***	a churn. a cardinal's red cap.
Un **bateleur*** Un **batelier***	a mountebank. a boatman, a ferryman.
Un **bâtiment***	(*a*) a building, an edifice. (*b*) a ship.
A **battalion**	(notice the spelling) un *bataillon*.
A **battle**	(notice the spelling) *une bataille*. A pitched battle, *une bataille rangée*. To fight a battle, *livrer bataille*.
Battre*	to beat. *Il a battu cet enfant*, he has beaten this child. *Battre froid*, to give the cold shoulder.
Se **battre***	(*a*) to beat one's self. (*b*) to fight. Ex.: *Cette armée s'est bien battue*, that army fought well.
Bâtir*	to build. *Il a bâti cette maison*, he has built this house.
A **bed**	(a piece of furniture) *un lit*. (a flower-bed) *une plate-bande, un massif, un parterre*.

Before . . . (of time) *avant*.
(of place) *devant*.
(meaning already) *déjà*. Ex.:
I have done this translation before, *J'ai déjà fait cette traduction*.

A bell . . . (a large bell) *une cloche*.
(a small bell) *une sonnette, une clochette*.
(a sledge bell) *un grelot*.
(of an alarm clock, &c.) *un timbre*.
A chime of bells, *un carillon*.
To ring the bell, *sonner*.

Une **berge*** . . . a steep bank.
Un **berger*** . . . a shepherd.
Une **bergère*** . . (*a*) a shepherdess.
(*b*) a kind of easy chair.
(*c*) a wagtail (a bird).

Bête* . . . (substantive) a beast.
Cet homme là, c'est ma bête noire,
I hate the sight of that man.
Une bête de somme, a beast of burden.
(adjective) stupid, silly. Ex.:
Qu'il est bête ! how stupid he his!

Bien* . . . (substantive) (*a*) good. Ex.: *Il cherche toujours à faire du bien aux autres*, he is always trying to do good to others.
(*b*) blessing, boon. Ex.: *La santé est un grand bien*, health is a great blessing.

Bien* (*continued*) . . (*c*) fortune. Ex.: *Il a perdu tout son bien au jeu*, he gambled his fortune away.

Un homme de bien, a good, honest, upright man.

(adverb) (*a*) well.

(*b*) very. Ex.: *Vous êtes bien bon*, you are very kind.

(*c*) at least. Ex.: *Il y a bien deux ans que je ne l'ai vu*, I have not seen him for at least two years.

(*d*) much, many. Ex.: *Il y avait bien du monde*, there were many people.

Il est bien dans ses affaires, he is well off, he is well to do.

C'est bien fait! It serves him right!

Être bien* . . . (*a*) to be good looking.

(*b*) to be comfortable. Ex.: *Asseyez-vous sur cette chaise vous serez mieux.—Non, merci, je suis très bien ici.*

Ils sont fort bien ensemble, they are on very good terms with each other.

Bière (fem.)* . . (*a*) beer.
(*b*) bier, coffin.

A bill . . . (bank) *un effet, un billet*.

(of a tradesman) *une facture, un compte, une note*.

(at a restaurant) *l'addition, la carte*.

(a placard) *une affiche*.

A **bill** (*continued*) . .	(parliament) *un projet de loi.* (of a bird) *un bec.* A bill of fare, *un menu.*
Un **billet*** . . .	(*a*) a ticket, (*b*) a note, a short letter.
A **billet** . . .	(a log) *une bûche.* (for quartering soldiers) *un billet de logement.*
To **bind** . . .	(to fasten) *lier, attacher.* (a book) *relier.* (a coat) *border.* (to compel) *lier, obliger, forcer.* Ex.: *Il est lié par sa promesse.*
A **bit** . . .	(a small piece) *un morceau.* (for a horse) *un mors.* He is not a bit sorry, *il n'est pas fâché le moins du monde.*
A **blade** . . .	(of a knife, of a sword) *une lame.* (of grass) *un brin (d'herbe).* (of an oar) *le plat (d'un aviron, d'une rame).*
Blesser* . . .	to wound.
To **bless** . .	*bénir.*
A **blessing** . .	(a benediction) *une bénédiction.* (a boon) *un bienfait, un bonheur.*
Blind . . .	(of one eye) *borgne.* (of both eyes) *aveugle.* (for windows) *un store.* Venetian blind, *une jalousie.*

To **blot** . . .	(with ink) *faire un pâté, faire une tache d'encre.* (to dry) *sécher.* To blot out, *effacer.*
Se **blottir*** . .	to squat, to crouch, to roll oneself up.
To **blow** . . .	(to breathe, to puff) *souffler.* (a horn, &c.) *sonner (du cor, &c.).* To blow up (by gunpowder) *faire sauter.* To blow down (by the wind) *renverser.* To blow out (candle, &c.) *souffler, éteindre (une bougie, &c.).* To blow out one's brains, *se faire sauter la cervelle* or *se brûler la cervelle.* The wind blows, *il fait du vent.* Full blown (flowers) *épanoui.*
Blue	(notice the spelling) *bl***eu**.
A **board** . . .	(a plank) *une planche.* (food) *la pension, la table.*
On **board** . . .	(navy) *à bord.*
To **board** . . .	(a ship) *aborder (un navire)* (to take someone as a boarder) *prendre quelqu'un en pension;* (to board at somebody's) *se mettre* (or *être*) *en pension chez quelqu'un.*
Bologne* . . .	a town in the north of Italy.
Boulogne* . .	a town in the north of France.

Un **bond***	a bound, a leap. *Prendre la balle au bond*, to seize time by the forelock. *Faire faux bond*, to fail anyone.
A **bond**	(a tie) *un lien*. (finances) *une obligation*. (of the customs) *un entrepôt*.
A **bone**	*un os*. (of a fish) *une arête*. A bone of contention, *une pomme de discorde*.
A **bonnet** Un **bonnet***	*un chapeau*. a woman's cap, or a man's cap, of soft material and without a peak. *Un gros bonnet*, a person of importance (familiar). *Avoir la tête près du bonnet*, to be hot-headed. *Ce sont deux têtes dans un bonnet*, they are hand and glove together. *C'est bonnet blanc et blanc bonnet*, it is six of one, and half-a-dozen of the other.
La **bonté*** A **bounty**	goodness, kindness. *une largesse, une gratification*.
Une **botte***	a Wellington boot. (*d'asperges*) a bundle (of asparagus). (*de foin*) a truss (of hay). (*escrime*) a thrust (fencing). *Chercher querelle à quelqu'un à propos de bottes*, to pick a quarrel with somebody about nothing, about a trifle.

Une **bouchée***	a mouthful.
Un **boucher***	a butcher.
Boucher*	(a) to stop up (a hole, an opening).
	(b) to cork (a bottle).
	Cet enfant est bouché, this child is stupid, not intelligent.

La **boue***	the mud.
Le **bout***	the end (*see* "end").

Un **boulet***	a cannon ball.
Une **boulette***	(a) (*de pain*) a pellet (*i.e*, a small piece of crumb rolled up with the fingers).
	(b) forced-meat ball.
	(c) a blunder (familiar), *il a fait une boulette,* he has put his foot in it.

A **bullet**	*une balle.*

Un **bouillon***	broth, beef-tea.
	Boire un bouillon, to swallow much water when swimming, *or* to lose a good deal of money.

Un **brouillon***	a rough copy, a rough draft (of a letter, etc.).
	Cet homme est un brouillon, that man is a meddling fellow, a busy body.

Un **bourgeois***	meant formerly a citizen, a burgess, a townsman; and now, it generally means a man belonging to the middle class.

Un **bourreau*** . . (*a*) a hangman, and executioner.
(*b*) a cruel man. Ex.: *Cet homme est un vrai bourreau*, that man is very cruel.

Un **bureau*** . . (*a*) an office (place of business). Ex.: *Je passerai à votre bureau à dix heures*, I will call at your office at ten o'clock.
(*b*) a bureau, a desk.

Un **bouton*** . . (*a*) a button.
(*b*) a bud.
(*c*) a pimple.
(*d*) a knob (of a lock).
Un bouton d'or, a butter-cup.

A **box** . . . (a fancy box) *une boîte*.
(for travelling) *une malle*.
(for alms) *un tronc*.
(a driver's seat) *un siège de cocher*.
(at the theatre) *une loge*.
(on the ear) *un soufflet, une gifle*.
(cash-box) *la caisse*.
(money-box) *une tirelire*.
(bonnet-box, hat-box) *un carton de chapeau* (or *à chapeau*).
(snuff-box) *une tabatière*.
(sentry-box) *une guérite*.
(Cristmas-box) *des étrennes*.
(paddle-box) *un tambour*.
(boxwood) *du buis*.
(boxing) *la boxe*.

A **branch** . . . (of a tree) *une branche*.
(of banks, &c.) *une succursale*.
To branch off (of trains), *bifurquer*.

Un **brasseur***	a brewer (not a brass worker).
Un **brosseur***	an officer's servant.
Une **bribe***	(*a*) a great lump of bread. (*b*) fragments of meat. (*c*) odd ends, scraps.
A **bribe**	*un présent (fait dans le but de corrompre).* To bribe, *acheter, corrompre, gagner, suborner.*
Une **bride***	a bridle. *Courir à bride abattue,* to ride at full speed, to tear along.
A **bride**	*une fiancée, une nouvelle mariée.*
Brilliant	(notice the spelling) *brillant.*
Une **bulle***	a bubble.
A **bull**	*un taureau.*
A **bunch**	(of keys) *un trousseau (de clefs).* (of grapes) *une grappe (de raisin).* (of flowers) *un bouquet.*
A **bundle**	(a parcel) *un paquet.* (of papers, banknotes, &c.) *une liasse.* (of asparagus) *une botte (d'asperges).* (of sticks) *un fagot.*
Butter*	to stumble (of horses).
To **butter**	*beurrer.*

C

Un **cahot***	(pronounce *kah-o*) jolt of a coach.
Le **chaos***	(pronounce *kah-o*) chaos.

Calico	(notice the spelling) *du calico*t.
Can	*pouvoir*.
	(meaning to know how to) *savoir*. Ex.: Can you swim? *savez-vous nager?*
Un canapé*	a sofa.
A canopy	*un dais* (pronounce "*day*").
Une cane* .	(feminine of *canard*) a duck.
Une canne*	a walking-stick.
A cannon .	(a military engine) *un canon*.
	(at billiards) *un carambolage*.
A canon .	(an ecclesiastic) *un chanoine*.
Un canonnier* .	a gunner.
Une canonnière*	(*a*) a gun-boat.
	(*b*) a pop-gun.
Un cap* . .	a cape (geography).
A cap . .	(woman's) *un bonnet*.
	(man's cap with a peak) *une casquette*.
	(man's cap without a peak and of soft material) *un bonnet*.
	(of fire-arms) *une capsule*.
	Cap-a-pie, *de pied en cap*.
Un capital* .	capital (money).
Une capitale* .	capital (town).
Un capon* .	(familiar) a coward.
A capon .	*un chapon*.
Le caractère* .	the temper. Ex.: *Cet homme a un mauvais caractère*, that man has a bad temper.

A **character**	(repute) *une réputation.* Ex.: That man has a bad character, *cet homme a une mauvaise réputation.* (at the theatre) *un rôle.* He is quite a character, *c'est un original.*
Care	(kind attentions) *soins* (plural). Ex.: Every care was bestowed upon him, *on le combla de soins.* Take care, *prenez garde.* With care (on parcels), *fragile.*
Cares	(anxiety) *souci.* Ex.: Cares have aged him, *les soucis l'ont vieilli.*
Un **carreau***	(*a*) a pane (of glass). (*b*) diamonds (at cards). (*c*) tile for the floor. *Rester sur le carreau,* to be killed on the spot.
A **carriage**	*une voiture.* A railway carriage, *un wagon.* A gun carriage, *un affût de canon.*
Un **carrier***. A **carrier**.	a quarry-man, a quarrier. *un voiturier, un camionneur.* (a bearer) *un porteur.*
Une **carte***	(*a*) a card. (*b*) a map. *Une carte de visite,* a visiting card. *Avoir carte blanche,* to have full power. *Tirer les cartes,* to tell fortunes with cards. *Perdre la carte,* to get disconcerted, to lose one's wits.
A **cart**	*une charrette.*

To **carve** . . .	(meat) *découper*.
	(stone, wood) *sculpter*.
Une **case*** . . .	(*a*) a negro's hut.
	(*b*) a pigeon-hole.
	(*c*) a square (chess-board).
A **case** . . .	(a box) *une caisse*.
	(a circumstance) *un cas*.
	(a suit in court) *une cause*.
	(a grammatical term) *un cas*.
	(an instance) *un exemple*.
	A book case, *une bibliothèque*.
	A needle case, *un étui à aiguilles*.
	A cigar case, *un porte-cigares*.
	A dressing case, *un nécessaire de toilette*.
	A jewel case, *un écrin*.
	A spectacle case, *un étui de lunettes*.
	An umbrella case, *un fourreau de parapluie*.
	A hat case, *un étui de chapeau*, (or *à chapeau*).
	A watch case, *une boîte de montre*.
	Should the case occur, *le cas échéant*.
Un **casque*** . .	a helmet.
A **cask** . . .	*un tonneau*.
Une **casquette*** .	a man's cap (*see* "cap").
A **casket** . . .	(for jewels) *un écrin*.
Causer* . . .	(*a*) to cause.
	(*b*) to chat.
	Nous avons causé de la pluie et du beau temps, we only talked about common-place subjects.

Une **caution*** . .	a bail, a security. *Un homme sujet à caution*, a man not to be trusted.
A **caution** . .	*un avis*, or *une précaution*.

Un **cavalier*** . .	(*a*) a horseman, a rider. (*b*) a male partner at a dance.
Un **chevalier*** . .	a knight. *Un chevalier d'industrie*, a swindler, one that lives by his wits.

Cavalry . . .	(notice the spelling) *la cavalerie*.

Une **cave*** . .	a cellar.
A **cave** . .	*une caverne*.

Celebrated . .	(famous) *célèbre*. Ex.: *Sa découverte l'a rendu célèbre*. (praised, extolled, sung) *célébré*. Ex.: *Les poètes ont célébré la naissance du prince*.

Censé* . .	supposed. Ex.: *Je suis censé ne pas savoir qu'il vous a écrit*.
Sensé* . .	sensible, intelligent. Ex.: *Cette remarque est très sensée*.

Un **cerf*** . .	a stag. *Un cerf volant*, a stag-beetle, a horn-beetle *or* a kite (toy).
Un **serf*** . .	a serf (a bondman, a slave).

La **chair***	flesh. *J'en ai la chair de poule*, it makes my flesh creep.
Une **chaire***	(*a*) a pulpit. (*b*) professorship (at a university).
A **chair**	*une chaise*.
Un **chandelier***	a candlestick.
A **chandelier**	*un lustre*.
Un **chanteur***	a singer.
Un **chantre***	a chorister (church).
Du **charbon***	coal, coals.
Un **chardon***	thistle.
Une **charge***	(*a*) a load, a burden. (*b*) a charge (of cavalry, &c.). (*c*) a caricature, exaggeration.
The **charge**	(the price) *le prix*.
Charger*	(*a*) to load (a gun, a cart, &c.). (*b*) to charge (a military term). *Se charger de*, to take upon one's self. Ex.: *Je me charge de le convaincre*.
To **charge**	(a price) *faire payer, prendre, compter*.
Une **chasse***	a hunt.
Une **châsse***	a reliquary.
Un **châssis***	a window frame, a garden frame.
Chasser*	(*a*) to shoot (game). (*b*) to expel, to turn out. *Chasser à courre*, to hunt, to course. *Chasser de race* (familiar), to take after one's parents.

Un **chat*** . . . a cat.

Il n'y avait pas un chat, there was not a soul there.

Il n'y a pas là de quoi fouetter un chat, it is not worth getting cross about.

Chat échaudé craint l'eau froide, a burnt child dreads the fire (proverb).

À bon chat, bon rat, set a thief to catch a thief; diamond cut diamond.

A **chat** . . . *une causerie.*

Chaud (and **froid**)* . (*a*) applied to **persons** and **animals,** are conjugated with **avoir.** Ex.: *Nous avons chaud.*

(*b*) applied to **things,** they take **être.** Ex.: *Cette eau est chaude.*

(*c*) when applied to the **weather,** the impersonal verb *il fait* must be used. Ex.: *Il fait chaud.* But if the word *temps* (weather) is used as the subject, *être* is required. Ex.: *Le temps était froid et humide.*

<small>Therefore the sentence, "The weather was fine," may be translated in two ways: **Il faisait** *beau temps,* or, *Le temps était beau* (**not** Le temps *faisait* beau). The reason of this rule is that *faire,* in this case, is (as stated above) an impersonal verb, and therefore can only have *il* for a subject, in the same way as *pleuvoir, neiger,* &c.</small>

Se **chauffer***	to warm one's self.
S'**échauffer***	to get excited (in a dispute, &c.).

A **chemist**	(a man learned in chemistry) *un chimiste*.
	(an apothecary) *un pharmacien*.

Un **chenil***	a dog kennel.
Une **chenille***	(*a*) caterpillar.
	(*b*) chenille (a kind of silk cord).

The **chest**	(of man) *la poitrine*.
	(of a horse) *le poitrail*.
	(a box) *un coffre, une caisse*.

Une **cheville***	(*a*) a peg.
	(*b*) ankle-bone.
	Se fouler la cheville, to sprain one's ankle.

Un **chœur***	(*a*) a choir (church).
	(*b*) a chorus.
	Un enfant de chœur, a chorister boy (church).
Un **cœur***	a heart.
	Avoir mal au cœur, to feel sick (to be affected with nausea).

A **church**	*une église*.
	(a Protestant church in Roman Catholic countries) *un temple*.

A **clock**	*une horloge*.
	(on a mantlepiece) *une pendule*.

Une **claie***	a hurdle.
Clay	*argile* (f.), *terre glaise* (f.).

Coasser*	to croak (of frogs).
Croasser*	to caw (of crows, ravens).

Du **coco*** . . .	liquorice-root water (a beverage).
Cocoa . . .	du cacao.
Cocoa-nut . .	une noix de coco.

Coffee . . . . (notice the spelling) du ca**fé**.

Un **coin*** . . .	(a) a corner. (b) a wedge.
Un **coing*** . .	a quince.
A **coin** . . .	(money) une pièce de monnaie.

Un **col*** . . .	a collar (of a shirt).
De la **colle*** . .	glue, paste.

A **collar** . . . (of a coat) un collet.
                           (of a shirt) un col.
                           (a detached collar) un faux col.
                           (a stand up collar) un col droit.
                           (a turned down collar) un col rabattu.
                           (of a dog) un collier.
                                  (Un collier means also a necklace).

A **collection** . . (of shells, stamps, &c.) une collection.
                           (in a church) une quête.
                           (post office) une levée.

Un **colon*** . . .	a colonist.
A **colon** . . .	(punctuation) deux points.

Une **commande*** . . an order (commerce).
                           Une maladie de commande, a feigned sickness.
                           Des louanges de commande, forced praises.

A **command** . . un commandement, un ordre.

Commander*	(*a*) to command. (*b*) to bespeak, to order. Ex.: *J'ai commandé le diner pour sept heures*, I have ordered the dinner for seven o'clock.
A **committee**	(notice the spelling) *un comité*. *Nous serons en petit comité*, we shall be a small party of friends.
Commode*	(substantive) a chest of drawers. (adjective) handy, convenient.
Commodité (fem.)* **Commodity**	convenience. *marchandise*.
A **companion**	(notice the spelling) *un compagnon.* (fem. *compagne*).
A **company**	(notice the spelling) *une compa***gnie**. We shall have company to-night, *nous aurons du monde ce soir*.
Une **complainte*** A **complaint**	a plaintive ballad. (an illness) *une maladie*. (lamentation) *une plainte*. To lodge a complaint, *porter plainte*.
La **complexion*** **Complexion**	constitution (of a person). *le teint*.
Comprendre*	(*a*) to understand. (*b*) to comprise, to include.

Un **compte***	. .	an account, a bill.
Un **comte***	. .	a count, an earl.
Un **comté***	. .	a county, a shire.
Un **conte***	. .	a story, a tale.
		Un vrai conte, an improbable story, a falsehood.

Un **concours*** . . (*a*) a competition, a competitive examination.
(*b*) co-operation, help. Ex.: *Son concours m'a été fort utile*, his co-operation, his help, has been very useful to me.
(*c*) a concourse of people, a great crowd (*une foule* or *une grande affluence* are more often used).
Un concours d'admission, an entrance examination.

Une **concussion***	.	peculation, exaction, embezzlement.
Concussion	. .	*un ébranlement, une secousse.* Concussion of the brain, *commotion cérébrale.*
Condolence	. .	(notice the spelling) *condoléance.*
Un **confectionneur***	.	a clothier.
A **confectioner**	.	*un confiseur.*
Une **confidence***	.	a secret entrusted to some one.
The **confidence**	.	*la confiance.*
Une **congrégation***	.	a religious order, a brotherhood.
A **congregation**	.	*une assemblée de fidèles.*
To **conquer**	. .	(persons) *vaincre.* (countries) *conquérir.*

Un **conservatoire*** .	an academy of music.
A **conservatory** .	*une serre.*

Consigner* . . .	(*a*) to consign. (*b*) to confine to the barracks (military term).

To **consume** . .	(fuel) *consumer.* (food) *consommer.*

Contenir* . . .	to contain.
Se **contenir*** . .	to repress one's feelings, to restrain oneself.

Les **convenances** (fem.)*	propriety, good manners.
Convenience . .	*commodité.* Do it at your convenience, *faites-le quand vous le pourrez,* or *quand vous aurez le temps.*

A **copy** . . .	(of a manuscript) *une copie.* (of books) *un exemplaire.* (for drawing) *un modèle.*

Une **corbeille*** . .	a basket. *Une corbeille de mariage,* wedding presents given by the bridegroom.
Une **corneille*** . .	a crow, a rook.

Une **corde*** . . .	a rope. *Usé jusqu'à la corde,* threadbare worn out. *Sauter à la corde,* to skip.
Un **cordon*** . .	a cord. *Un cordon bleu,* a very good woman cook.

Une **corne*** . . .	(*a*) a horn.
	(*b*) a dog's ear (on the leaves of a book).
Some **corn** . .	(wheat) *du blé, du froment*.
A **corn** . . .	(on the foot) *un cor au pied*.
Correspondence .	(notice the spelling) *une correspondance*.
Une **côte*** . . .	(*a*) sea-coast, shore.
	(*b*) hill, declivity, slope.
	(*c*) rib.
Un **côté*** . . .	a side.
	Un point de côté, a stitch (a pain) in the side.
	À côté de, by the side of.
	Du côté de, in the direction of.
	De côté, sideways, obliquely, aslant.
	Mettre de côté, to put aside.
	Mettre à côté de, to put by the side of.
	La chambre à côté, the next room.
La **cote*** . . .	quotation (stock exchange).
Some **cotton** . .	(notice the spelling) *du coton*.
Un **cou*** . . .	a neck.
	Un cou-de-pied, instep.
Un **coup*** . . .	a blow, a knock.
	Un coup de pied, a kick.
	Un coup de tonnerre, a clap of thunder.
	Un coup de vent, a gust of wind.
	Un coup d'air, a slight cold caught in a draught.
	Un coup de feu, a shot.
	Un coup de coude, a nudge.
	Un coup de dent, a bite.

Un **coup*** (*continued*)

Un coup de Jarnac, a treacherous blow[1].
Un coup de tête, a rash action.
Un coup d'œil, a glance.
Un coup de soleil, a sun stroke.
Un coup de sifflet, a whistle, (a shrill sound made by whistling).
Un coup de sang, a congestion of the brain.
Un coup d'essai, a first attempt.
Un coup de maître, a masterly stroke.
Un coup de sonnette, a pull at the bell.
Le coup de l'étrier, the parting glass, the stirrup cup.
Un coup monté, a got-up affair.
Tout à coup, suddenly, unexpectedly.
Tout d'un coup, at once, all at once.
Encore un coup, once more.
A coup sûr, to a certainty.
Par un coup de hasard, by a mere chance.
Pour le coup vous avez tort, well, now you are wrong.
Sans coup férir, without striking a blow.
Être aux cent coups, to be half frantic with anxiety, with sorrow.
Boire un coup, to have something to drink.

---

[1] Gui Chabot, seigneur de Jarnac, dans un duel célèbre, en présence de toute la cour (1547) blessa la Châtaigneraie, son adversaire, au jarret d'un coup inattendu, de là "coup de Jarnac," coup donné par trahison.

Un **coup*** (*continued*)	*Donner un coup de main à,* to give a hand, a help. *Donner un coup de collier,* to put one' shoulder to the wheel. *Faire d'une pierre deux coups,* to kill two birds with one stone.
The **country**	(not the capital) *la province.* Ex.: *La province cherche à imiter la capitale.* (not the town) *la campagne.* Ex.: *Il a passé ses vacances à la campagne.* (the whole country) *le pays.* Ex.: *L'Angleterre est un pays très riche.* (the mother country) *la patrie.*
Countryman	(a rustic) *un paysan, un campagnard.* (of the same country) *un compatriote.* what countryman is he? *de quel pays est-il?*
La **cour***	(*a*) court (of a Sovereign). (*b*) courtyard. *Eau bénite de cour,* empty promises, fair words and nothing else.
Le **cours***	(*a*) course (of lectures, of streams, &c.). (*b*) rate of exchange. *Donner cours à sa fureur,* to give vent to one's rage.

La **course***	race, running. *Prendre un fiacre à la course*, to engage a cab by the distance—that is, to pay the fare according to the distance travelled, not by the hour.
A **courier**	(notice the spelling) *un courrier*.
Un **courtier***	a broker. *Un courtier maritime*, a ship-broker.
A **courtier**	*un courtisan*.
Un **cousin***	(*a*) a cousin. *Un cousin germain*, a first cousin. (*b*) a gnat.
Un **coussin***	a cushion.
Un **crâne***	a skull. *Faire le crâne*, to swagger.
A **crane**	(a bird *or* a machine for raising heavy weights) *une grue*.
Un **crêpe***	crape.
Une **crêpe***	a pancake.
Cricket	(insect) *un grillon*. (game) *le cricket*.
To **cross**	(a street, &c.) *traverser* (*une rue* &c.) (the arms) *croiser* (*les bras*). To cross out, off, *effacer, rayer*. To cross the threshold, *franchir le seuil*. To be cross, (to be in a bad temper), *être de mauvaise humeur*.

Une **crosse*** .	. .	(*a*) a butt end (of a gun). (*b*) a bishop's crosier.
A **cross** .	. .	*une croix*.

Cru* . .	. .	(*a*) raw. (*b*) believed, thought, (participle of *croire*).
Crû*	. .	grown (participle of *croître*).

To **cry** .	. .	(to shout), *crier*. (to exclaim), *s'écrier*. (to weep), *pleurer*.

Du **cuir***	. .	leather, hide. *Faire des cuirs*, faults made by uneducated French people, and consisting in sounding *s* for *t*, or vice versâ, when running words together, or in pronouncing these letters although they do not occur in the words used: as *Ils étaient* **z**ici, *Je l'ai vu* **z**aujourd'hui for *Ils étaient ici, Je l'ai vu aujourd'hui*. A fault somewhat similar to that made in English when the *h* is dropped.
Du **cuivre***	. .	copper.

Cuire* .	. .	(*a*) to cook. (*b*) to smart. Ex.: *La main me cuit*, my hand smarts. *Il vous en cuira*, you shall smart for that.

Un **culte*** .	. .	(*a*) worship, adoration. (*b*) religion, creed.
Une **culture*** .	.	cultivation.

Un curé*	a vicar, a rector, a parish priest
A curate	*un vicaire.*
La curée*	quarry (game killed).
Curer*	to cleanse (a well, &c.)
To cure	*guérir.*
	(meat) *saler, mariner.*

D

Un dada*	a "gee-gee" (baby talk). *C'est son dada,* it is his hobby.
A dada	*un papa.*
A dance	(notice the spelling) *une danse.*
Dark	(of colours) *foncé.* Ex.: A dark blue ribbon, *un ruban bleu foncé.*
	(of hair) *brun, châtain,* or *noir,* Ex.: His hair is dark, *il a les cheveux noirs.*
	(of complexion) *brun.*
	(of clouds) *noir.*
	It is dark at five o'clock, *il fait nuit;* or *il fait sombre à cinq heures.*
A date	(time) *une date.*
	(a fruit) *une datte.*
	(on medals and coins) *le millésime.*
	Out of date, (old fashioned) *suranné.*
Débattre*	(active verb) to discuss, to debate, to argue.
Se débattre*	to struggle, to resist.

The **deck** . . .	*le pont, le tillac.*
	The quarter-deck, *le gaillard d'arrière.*
	The fore-deck, *le gaillard d'avant.*
To **deck** . . .	*orner, parer.*
Deep	*profond.*
	(of colours) *foncé.*
	(of sound) *grave.*
	A deep voice, *une voix de basse.*
	In deep mourning, *en grand deuil.*
Défaire* . . .	to undo.
Se **défaire de*** .	to get rid of.
Defective . . .	*défectueux.*
	(of verbs) *défectif.*
A **defence** . . .	(notice the spelling) *une défense.*
Défendre* . . .	(*a*) to defend, to protect.
	(*b*) to forbid. Ex.: *Je vous le défends,* I forbid you to do it.
	Il ne s'en défend pas, he does not deny it.
La **défiance*** . .	distrust, mistrust.
A **defiance** . .	*un défi.*
Défier* . . .	to defy, to challenge.
Se **défier de*** . .	to mistrust, to suspect.
Dégoûter* . . .	to disgust.
Dégoutter* . .	to trickle, to drip.
To **deign** . . .	(notice the spelling) *daigner.*
Délayer* . . .	to dilute.
To **delay** . . .	*retarder, remettre, différer.*

Democracy	(notice the spelling) *la démocratie* (pronounce democracie).
Une **demoiselle***	(*a*) a young lady. (*b*) a dragon-fly. (*c*) a paving beetle, (a tool).
Le **dénoument***	the denouement, (the winding-up of plays, novels, &c.).
Le **dénûment***	destitution, poverty.
Une **dent***	a tooth. *Avoir les dents longues*, to be famished. *Avoir une dent contre quelqu'un*, to have a grudge against someone. *Être sur les dents*, to be tired out.
A **dent**	*une coche, un creux.*
Départir*	to distribute, to divide.
Se **départir de***	to abandon, to give up.
To **depart**	*partir, s'en aller.*
Déportements (m. pl.)*	dissolute conduct.
Deportment	*maintien, manières.*
Se **dérider***	to unbend one's brow, to cheer up.
To **deride**	*railler, tourner en dérision.*
Dérober*	to rob, to steal.
Se **dérober***	to steal away, to escape, to disappear, to hide one's-self. *Se dérober à la justice*, to fly (to hide) from justice.
To **disrobe**	*déshabiller*, or *se déshabiller.*

Désirer* . . .	to wish.
To **desire**. . .	(somebody to do something), *prier quelqu'un de faire quelque chose*, or *ordonner à quelqu'un de faire quelque chose.*
Un **dessin*** . . .	a drawing.
Un **dessein*** . .	a design. *À dessein*, on purpose, intentionally.
Une **destitution*** .	dismissal, removal from office.
Destitution . .	(poverty) *le dénûment, l'indigence, la misère.* (abandon) *un abandon.*
Déterrer* . . .	to unearth (*i.e.* to disinter *or* to find out, to discover).
To **deter** . . .	*empêcher, dissuader, retenir.*
Un **devis*** . . .	an estimate (builder's, architect's, &c.).
Une **devise*** . .	a motto.
A **device** . . .	*un plan, un moyen, un stratagème.*
The **dew** . . .	*la rosée.* The evening dew, *le serein.*
A **diamond** . . .	(a precious stone) *un diamant.* (at cards) *un carreau.*
A **dictionary** . .	(notice the spelling) *un dictionnaire.*
La **diète*** . . .	low diet. *Faire diète*, to eat nothing, *or* very little (according to the doctor's orders).
A **diet** . . .	*un régime.*

Un **différend*** . .	a dispute, a quarrel. *Avoir un différend avec quelqu'un,* to be at variance with some one.
Différent*	different.
Différer* . . .	(*a*) to defer, to delay. (*b*) to differ. *Cela diffère du tout au tout,* that is entirely different, it is quite another question.
A **dinner** . . .	(notice the spelling) *un dîner*.
To **direct** . . .	(a person) *diriger, renseigner, indiquer le chemin.* (a letter) *adresser (une lettre).*
Directement* . . **Directly** . . .	in a straight line. *immédiatement, tout de suite.*
Disappointment. .	(notice the spelling) *un d**é**sappoint**e**ment.*
Disaster . . .	(notice the spelling) *un d**é**sastre.*
To **discharge** . .	(a servant) *congédier, renvoyer.* (from prison) *libérer, élargir.* (a debt) *acquitter, payer.* (arrows) *décocher, lancer.* (fire-arms) *faire feu, tirer.* (a duty) *s'acquitter de, accomplir.*
A **disgrace** . . .	(disfavour) *une disgrâce.* Ex.: *Il est en disgrâce à la cour.* (shame) *une honte.* Ex.: It is a disgrace to the nation, *c'est une honte pour la nation.*

Disillusion	(notice the spelling) *une désillusion.*
A disinfectant	(notice the spelling) *un désinfectant.*
Se disputer*	to quarrel, to wrangle.
To dispute	*discuter.*
Distraire*	to amuse.
To distract	*bouleverser, rendre fou de douleur.*
Diviser*	to divide.
To devise	*imaginer, inventer.*
To divide	(arithmetic) *diviser.* (to distribute) *distribuer, partager.* (to separate) *séparer.*
A door	*une porte.* (of a carriage) *une portière.* Folding doors, *porte à deux battants.* Back-door, *porte de derrière.* Indoors, *à la maison,* or *chez soi.* Out of doors, *dehors,* or *en plein air.*
Une dot*	(pronounce *dott*) a marriage portion, a dowry.
A dot	*un point.*
Doter*	to give a dowry, to endow.
To dote	*radoter.*
To dote on	*aimer éperdument, aimer à la folie, raffoler de.*
A doubt	(notice the spelling) *un doute.*

Douter* . . . to doubt. Ex.: *Je doutais de son courage*, I doubted his courage.

Se douter* . . to suspect, to surmise rightly. Ex.: *Je me doutais de son courage*, I thought he would be courageous (and he proved so).—*Je me doutais qu'il viendrait*, I suspected he would come. *Je m'en doutais bien!* I thought so!

Draught . . . (of air) *un courant d'air*.
(a dose of medicine) *une potion*.
(drawing) *une esquisse, une ébauche*.
(depth of water) *un tirant (d'eau)*.
(rough copy) *un brouillon*.
A game of draught, *un jeu de dames*.
To drink at a draught, *boire d'un trait, d'un coup*.

Dresser* . . . (a) to erect, to raise. *Dresser une échelle*, to raise a ladder.
(b) to lay (a snare), *dresser un piège*.
(c) to draw up (a report), *dresser un rapport*.
(d) to prick up (the ears), *dresser les oreilles*.
(e) to pitch (a tent), *dresser une tente*.
(f) to train (animals), *dresser un chien*, but "to train" a race-horse is *entrainer un cheval*.

Se **dresser*** . . to stand on end. Ex.: *Mes cheveux se dressaient d'épouvante*, my hair stood on end with terror.

To **dress** . . . (to clothe) *habiller, s'habiller*.
(food) *accommoder*.
(wound) *panser (une blessure)*.
(a military term) *aligner*.
Right dress! *A droite alignement!*

To **drive** . . . *conduire*. Ex.: Can you drive? *Savez-vous conduire?*
(for pleasure) *se promener en voiture*.
To drive to a place, *aller en voiture à*.
To drive (so many miles), *faire (tant de kilomètres) en voiture*.
To drive mad, *rendre fou*,

Droit* . . . . (adjective, adverb) straight. Ex.: *Une ligne droite*, a straight line.
(substantive) right. Ex.: *C'est son droit*, it is his right.
Faire son droit, to study for the law.
Il fera droit à votre demande, He will accede to your claim. He will grant your request.
Les droits de douane, custom-house duties.
Le droit des gens, the law of nations.

Drôle* . . . . (subst.) a rascal, a scoundrel.
(adj.) droll, funny.
C'est un drôle de corps (familiar) he is a queer fellow.

To **drop**	(neuter verb) *tomber*. (active verb) *laisser tomber*. Ex.: He dropped his plate, *il laissa tomber son assiette*. To drop a letter in the post, *jeter une lettre à la poste*.
A **drum**	*un tambour*. (of the ear) *le tympan*. The big drum, *la grosse caisse*. A kettle-drum, *une timbale*.
Dur*	hard.
Durcir*	to harden.
Durer*	to last.

E

An **ear**	*une oreille*. (of corn) *un épi*.
Early	(in the day) *de bonne heure, de bon matin*. Ex.: He always rises early, *il se lève toujours de bonne heure*, or *de bon matin*. Come early, *venez de bonne heure*. (in the month, in the century, &c.), *au commencement du mois, du siècle, etc.* (horticulture) *hâtif*.
East	(cardinal point) *l'est* (the " t " is sounded). (Eastern countries) *l'Orient*. The Far East, *l'extrême Orient*. My room faces the East, *ma chambre est au levant*. — <small>*Levant* means also the Eastern shores of the Mediterranean: the Levant.</small>

Eccentric	(notice the spelling) *excentrique*.
Une **écharde***	a splinter.
Une **écharpe***	(*a*) a scarf. (*b*) a sling for the arm. Ex.: *Il a le bras en écharpe*, he has his arm in a sling.
Écharper*	to slash, to cut to pieces. Ex.: *Le régiment fut écharpé*, the regiment was cut to pieces.
Éclaircir*	to clear up (mystery, weather). Ex.: *Le temps s'éclaircit*, the weather is clearing up.
Éclairer*	to light, to give light. Ex.: *Cette lampe éclaire bien*. *Éclairez Monsieur*, show a light to the gentleman. *Éclairer une armée*, to cover the front of a army by scouting.
Un **éclat***	(*a*) eclat. (*b*) splinter (of wood, stone, &c.) Ex.: *Voler en éclats*, to fly into splinters. (*c*) glitter, brightness, glare. Ex.: *On ne peut soutenir l'éclat du soleil*, one cannot bear the glare of the sun. *Un éclat de rire*, a burst of laughter.
Economical	(of persons) *économe*. (of things) *économique*.
Un **écran***	a screen.
Un **écrin***	a jewel case, a casket.

The **edge**	*le bord.* (of swords, knives) *le fil, le tranchant.* (of books) *la tranche.* (of forests) *la lisière.* To set one's teeth on edge, *agacer les dents, faire grincer les dents.*
Un **éditeur*** An **editor**	a publisher. (of newspapers), *un rédacteur, un gérant.*
Élever*	(*a*) to raise. Ex.: *Élever la voix.* (*b*) to bring up (children). (*c*) to breed, to rear (animals).
S'**élever***	(*a*) to ascend. (*b*) to amount (of accounts).
Se **lever***.	to get up; to stand up.
S'**embraser*** **Embrasser***	to take fire, to kindle. (*a*) to kiss. (*b*) to embrace, to comprise, to include.
Emporter* S'**emporter***	to carry away, to take away. (of persons) to fly into a passion. Ex.: *Il s'emporte pour un rien.* (of horses) to run away, to bolt.
En*	The definite article is omitted after *en* (Ex.: *En France*) except in the following locutions: *En l'absence de, en l'air, en l'an, en l'année, en l'honneur de.* <small>Notice that although the article is used in *en l'air*, as "*il jeta sa casquette* (cap) *en l'air,*" it is dropped in the locution *en plein air*, in the open air.</small>

The **end**	(the conclusion, the ending) *la fin.* Ex.: *La fin d'un livre.* (the extremity) *le bout.* Ex.: *le bout d'un bâton.* (object, design) *le but.* Ex.: He attained his end, *il est parvenu à son but.* At the end of two months, *au bout de deux mois.* To put an end to, *mettre fin à,* or *mettre un terme à.*
An **enemy**	(notice the spelling) *un ennemi.*
Enfouir*	to hide in the ground.
S'enfuir*	to flee, to take to flight.
Engager*	(*a*) to induce, to advise. (*b*) to pledge. *Engager le combat,* to begin the fight.
S'engager*	(*a*) to promise. (*b*) to enlist.
To **engage**	(a carriage) *arrêter, retenir, louer.* (a servant) *arrêter, retenir.* To be engaged (bethrothed), *être fiancé.*
An **engineer**	(*a*) *un ingénieur.* (*b*) (in the army) *un soldat du génie,* or *un officier du génie.*
S'engraver*	to run in a sandbank (of boats).
To **engrave**	*graver.*
Ennuyant*	annoying.
Ennuyeux*	(*a*) tiresome. (*b*) tedious.

Enragé*	mad (of dogs).
	Faire enrager, to tease.
Enraged	*furieux*.

Un **enseigne***	un ensign (an officer).
Une **enseigne***	(*a*) an ensign (a flag).
	(*b*) a sign-board.
	Être logé à la même enseigne, to be in the same predicament.

Entendre*	to hear.
	Qu'entendez-vous par cela? What do you mean by that?
	J'entends que vous restiez ici, I wish (I order) you to stay here.
	Faites comme vous l'entendez, do as you please.
	Il n'entend pas raillerie, he cannot take a joke.
	Il n'entend rien aux affaires, he knows nothing about business.
	Entendre à demi-mot, to know how to take a hint.
	Bien entendu! of course, to be sure!
S'entendre*	(*a*) to hear one another.
	(*b*) to agree. Ex.: *Ils ne peuvent pas s'entendre*, they cannot agree.
	Cela s'entend, that is understood, that is a matter of course.

To **enter**	(a room, &c.) *entrer* **dans** (*une chambre*).
	(to write down) *inscrire, enregistrer*.

Entraîner*	(*a*) to drag away, to hurry away.
	(*b*) to train (race-horses).
	La guerre entraîne après elle bien des maux, war entails many evils.
An **envelope**	(notice the spelling) *une enve-lo**pp**e.*
Un **épagneul***	a spaniel.
Un **Espagnol***	a Spaniard.
Une **épreuve***	(*a*) a test.
	(*b*) an ordeal.
	(*c*) a printer's proof.
	A l'épreuve de, proof against.
Une **preuve***	a proof.
Un **équipage***	(*a*) an equipage, a carriage.
	(*b*) a crew (of a ship).
Ermine	(notice the spelling) **h***ermine* (fem.).
Esprit (mas.)*	(*a*) mind.
	(*b*) ghost.
	(*c*) wit.
	(*d*) spirit (of wine, &c.).
	Un esprit follet, a goblin.
	Avoir de l'esprit, to be witty.
	Faire de l'esprit, to play the wit.
Estimer*	(*a*) to esteem.
	(*b*) to estimate.
Etiquette (fem.)*	(*a*) etiquette.
	(*b*) label.

Un **étranger***	(a) a stranger. (b) a foreigner. *Voyager à l'étranger*, to travel abroad.
Exaggeration	(notice the spelling) *une exagération*.
Exalté*	(a) exalted. (b) nervously excited.
An **examination**	*un examen*.
An **examiner**	*un examinateur*.
An **example**	(notice the spelling) *un exemple*.
Exaucer*	to hearken to, to grant. Ex.: *Dieu exaucera vos prières*, God will give ear to your prayers.
Exhausser*	to raise, to make higher (architecture).
To **exhaust**	*épuiser*.
An **exercise**	*un exercice*. (a translation into a foreign language) *un thème*. (a translation from a foreign language) *une version*. *Faire l'exercice* (soldiers), to be drilled.
Exile	(notice the spelling) *un exil*.
Expansif*	communicative.
Expensive	*cher, coûteux*.
Une **expérience***	(a) experience. (b) an experiment.

D 2

An **explorer**	*un explorateur*.
Exprès*	on purpose. Ex.: *Il l'a fait exprès*, he did it on purpose.
Expressément*	expressly.
Exquisite	(nice) *exquis*. (of pain) *atroce*.
Extravagant	(unreasonable) *extravagant*. (prodigal) *dépensier, prodigue*. (of prices) *exorbitant, fou*.

F

Une **fabrique***	(*a*) a vestry-board. (*b*) a manufactory. *Au prix de fabrique*, at cost price.
A **fabric**	(cloth) *une étoffe*.
The **face**	*le visage, la face, la figure*. (of a watch) *le cadran*. To make faces, *faire des grimaces*.
Être **fâché***	(*a*) to be offended. (*b*) to be angry. (*c*) to be sorry.
Un **facteur***	(*a*) a postman. (*b*) a porter (at railway stations). *Un facteur de pianos*, a piano maker. *Un facteur d'orgues*, an organ-builder.
Une **facture***	a bill (tradesman's).

Fade*	unsavoury, tasteless.
Faded	(of flowers, &c.) *fané, flétri, passé.*

To fail	*manquer.* Ex. : He failed to do his duty, *il a manqué à son devoir.*—Come without fail, *venez sans manquer.*
	(commerce) *faire faillite.*
	(in an undertaking) *échouer.*
	(in an examination) *échouer, être refusé, ne pas passer.*

Faire*	to make, to do.
	Faire une promenade, to take a walk.
	Faire dix milles, to walk ten miles.
	Faire l'aumône, to give alms.
	Faire des armes, to fence.
	Faire le malade, to sham illness.
	Faire la sourde oreille, to pretend not to hear, to refuse to take the hint.
	Faire mine de, or *Faire semblant de*, to pretend to.
	Faire bonne mine à mauvais jeu, to put a good face on the matter.
	Faire bonne chère, to eat good things, to live well.
	Faire cas, to value, to appreciate.
	Faire pitié, to excite pity.
	Se faire à, to get accustomed to.
	Se faire mal, to hurt one's self.
	Comment cela se fait-il? how is that? how do you account for it?

Faire* (*continued*) . Que voulez-vous que j'y fasse? how can I help it?
Je n'ai que faire de vos conseils, I do not want your advice.
Qu'est-ce que cela fait? what does it matter?
Qu'est-ce que cela vous fait? what is that to you?
Cela ne me fait rien, I do not mind, it does not matter to me.
Il se fait tard, it is getting late (in the day).
Un homme fait, a grown-up man.

Ne **faire que*** . . to do nothing but. Ex.: *Il ne fait que sortir et rentrer*, he does nothing but go out and in.

Ne **faire que de*** . to have just. Ex.: *Il ne fait que de sortir*, he has just gone out.

Family . . . (notice the spelling) *une famille*, (notice that words derived from *famille* are spelt with one l. Ex.: *familier, familiarité*.

La **fange*** . . . mire, mud.
A **fang** . . . (of dogs) *un croc* (pronounce *cro*).
(of boars) *une défense*.

Fast . . . . (quick) *rapide*.
(of colours) *bon teint*
It is raining fast, *il pleut à verse*.
To hold fast, *tenir ferme*.

Fastidieux*	irksome, dull. *Une lecture fastidieuse*, a "dry" reading.
Fastidious	*difficile.*
Un **fat***	(pronounce *un fatt*) a fop, a coxcomb.
Fat	(stout) *gros, gras.*
Un **faux***	a forgery.
Une **faux***	a scythe.
Des **favoris***	(*a*) favourites. (*b*) whiskers.
Femelle*	female (is applied *only* to animals in French).
Fendre*	to split.
Fondre*	to melt.
Fonder*	to found.
Une **ferme***	a farm.
Ferme (adj.)*	firm (adj.).
A **firm**	*une maison de commerce.*
Feu (mas.)*	(substantive) fire. *Le feu grisou*, fire-damp. *Un feu de joie*, feu-de-joie (a military term) *or* a bonfire. *Un feu d'artifice*, fireworks. *Un coup de feu*, a shot. *Un feu follet*, a Will-o'-the-wisp. *Faire long feu* (military), to hang fire. (adjective) late, deceased. (*Feu* is invariable when it is placed before the article, but agrees when placed after. Ex.: *Feu la reine, la feue reine*).

La **figure***	the face.
Figure	(of a person) *la taille, la tournure.*
	(a cipher) *un chiffre.*

Fil (mas.)*	(*a*) a thread.
	(*b*) edge (of a knife, &c.).
	(*c*) wire.
	Du fil de fer, iron wire.
	Du fil de laiton, brass wire.
	Un fil à plomb, a plumb-line.
	Aller contre le fil, to go against the grain.
	Passer au fil de l'épée, to put to the sword.

Une **file***	a row, a file.
	Marcher à la file, to walk one behind the other, to march in file.
	Par file à droite! right wheel! (a military term).
A **file**	(a tool) *une lime.*
	(of bills, &c.) *une liasse.*
	(of documents) *un dossier.*
	(of newspapers) *une collection.*
To **file**	(to rub with a file) *limer.*
To **file past**	(to march past) *défiler.*

Filer*	(*a*) to spin.
	(*b*) to be off.
	Filer doux, to be all submission, to put up with an insult.

Fire	*du feu.*
	(a conflagration) *un incendie.*
	To miss fire (fire-arms), *rater.*
	He will not set the Thames on fire, *il n'a pas inventé la poudre.*

To **fire**	(to set on fire) *mettre le feu à*. (to shoot) *faire feu*, or *tirer un coup de fusil, de revolver*, etc. (see "to shoot"). I fired at him, *je lui ai tiré un coup de fusil, de revolver, etc.*
Un **flacon***	(*a*) a flask. (*b*) a scent-bottle.
Un **flocon***	(*a*) a flake (of snow). (*b*) a tuft (of wool).
A **flag**	(of the army) *un drapeau*. (of the navy) *un pavillon*. A flagstone, *une dalle*.
Une **flaque***	A puddle.
A **flake**	*un flocon*.
Flat	*plat*. (of wine, beer, &c.) *éventé*. (of music) *bémol*. (a storey of a house) *un étage*. A flat nose, *un nez camard, un nez camus*.
Une **fleur***	a flower. *A fleur de terre, à fleur d'eau*, even with, on a level with, the ground, the water, &c. *Être à la fleur de l'âge*, to be in the prime of one's life.
Les **flots***	waves, billows. *A flot*, afloat. *A flots*, in torrents, in streams, in great abundance.
Une **flotte***	a fleet.

DICTIONARY OF DIFFICULTIES.

To **fly**	(of birds, &c.) *voler*.
	(to run away) *s'enfuir*.
	To fly from justice, *se soustraire* (or *se dérober*) *à la justice*.
	To fly into a passion, *se mettre en colère*, or *s'emporter*.
	To fly in pieces, *voler en éclats*, or *éclater*.

La **foi***	the faith.
Le **foie***	the liver.
Une **fois***	once.
	Toutefois, however.
	Toutes les fois, everytime.

La **folie***	madness.
A **folly**	*une sottise*.

Un **fond***	(*a*) the further end, the extremity. Ex.: *Il est au fond du jardin*.
	(*b*) back-ground (of pictures).
	Faire fond sur, to depend upon.
	Couler à fond, to sink (of boats).
	A fond, thoroughly, perfectly. Ex.: *Il possède cette langue à fond*, he is thoroughly master of that language.
	Cette maison a brûlé de fond en comble, that house was burnt down.
	Il est ruiné de fond en comble, he is utterly ruined.
Fonds*	funds.
	Céder son fonds, to sell one's business.

For	(applied to time) *pendant.* Ex.: For a week, *pendant une semaine.*
Force (fem.)*	(substantive) strength. (adverb) much, a great many. Ex.: *Il nous fit force compliments,* he paid us a great many compliments. *A force de,* by dint of. *Force me fut de,* I was compelled to. *Faire force de voiles,* to crowd all sail.
Forcer*	to force, to compel. *Forcer le pas,* to hurry one's pace.
S'efforcer de*	to strive to, to do one's best to.
Un **foret***	a gimlet, a drill.
Une **forêt***	a forest.
Fort*	(*a*) strong. (*b*) hot (over-spiced). (*c*) fort, stronghold. *Un coffre-fort,* an iron safe. *Le plus fort est fait,* the hardest part (the most difficult part) is over. *Je me fais fort de le convaincre,* I feel confident of convincing him, I take upon myself to convince him. *Il est fort en mathématiques,* he knows mathematics well. *C'est trop fort,* or *c'est par trop fort!* It is too bad! *Dans le fort de l'hiver,* in the depth of winter. *Dans le fort du combat,* in the heat of the battle.

A **fortress**	(notice the spelling) *une forteresse*.
Une **fosse***	(*a*) a pit. (*b*) a grave.
Un **fossé***	(*a*) a ditch. (*b*) a moat.
Un **fou***	a madman. (at chess) a bishop.
A **fool**	*un sot, un idiot, un imbécile*. (a court-jester) *un fou, un bouffon*. Fool-hardy, *téméraire*.
Une **foule***	a crowd.
Fouler*	(*a*) to tread upon, to trample down, to trample under. (*b*) to sprain. Ex.: *Je me suis foulé la cheville*, I sprained my ankle.
Un **fourgon***	(*a*) a railway van. (*b*) a military waggon. (*c*) a poker. *La pelle* (shovel) *se moque de fourgon*, it is the kettle calling the pot black.
Un **foyer***	(*a*) a hearth. (*b*) a focus. *Le foyer des acteurs*, the green-room (theatre). *Le foyer du public*, the lobby (theatre). *Combattre pour ses foyers*, to fight for one's home.

Frais*.	(adjective) fresh. (substantive) expenses. *Faux frais,* incidental expenses.
Frame	(of a picture) *un cadre.* (of an umbrella) *la monture.* (of mind) *une disposition.*
Fréter*	to charter (a ship).
Fretter*	to bind (the head of a stake, &c., with an iron hoop to prevent it from splitting).
To **fret**	(to worry) *se tourmenter, se faire du mauvais sang.*
Friser*	(*a*) to curl (hair). (*b*) to graze (to touch lightly).
Un **frison***	a curl.
Un **frisson***	shivering, shiver. *Cela donne le frisson,* that makes one shudder.
Le **front***	the forehead. *Marcher de front,* to walk abreast. *Il a eu le front de me rire au nez,* he had the impudence to laugh in my face.
The **front**.	(of a house) *le devant, la façade.* (of a shop) *la devanture.* A front room, *une chambre sur le devant.*
La **fumée***	smoke.
Le **fumet***	odour of cooked meat, &c.
Le **fumier***	manure.

Fumer[*]	(*a*) to smoke. (*b*) to manure.
Furniture	(a piece of furniture) *un meuble*, (the whole of the furniture), *le mobilier, les meubles, l'ameublement*.
Fourniture[*]	A supply, provisions, goods.
Fus[*]	*Je m'en fus,* I went away; *il s'en fut,* he went away. <small>The verb *être* is sometimes used instead of *aller*, but only in the preterite (*passé défini*).</small>
The **future**	(grammatical term) *le futur*. (time to come) *l'avenir*. Ex.: *On ne peut prévoir l'avenir,* the future cannot be foreseen.

G

A **gale**.	*une tempête*.
La **gale**[*].	mange.
Gallant	(to ladies) *galant*. (courageous) *courageux, brave, vaillant*.
A **gallery**	(notice the spelling) *une galerie*.
Gallop	(notice the spelling) *un galop*.
Un **galon**[*]	(*a*) a stripe (on soldiers' sleeves). (*b*) a narrow gold or silver lace.
A **gallon**	*Mesure valant un peu plus de quatre litres et demi.*

Un **garçon***	(*a*) a boy. (*b*) a waiter. (*c*) a bachelor (an unmarried man). *Un garçon boulanger, un garçon boucher, etc.*, a journeyman baker, journeyman butcher, &c.
Un **garde***	(*a*) a keeper. (*b*) a guardsman. *Un corps de garde*, a guard-house. *Un garde du corps*, a life-guard.
Une **garde***	(*a*) a sick-nurse. (*b*) a hilt of a sword.
Garder*	(*a*) to keep. (*b*) to tend (cattle). (*c*) to nurse (the sick). (*d*) to guard.
Se **garder de***	to take care not to. Ex.: *Gardez-vous de faire cela*, take care not to do that.
Un **gardien***	(*a*) a keeper. (*b*) a warder (prison).
A **guardian**	*un tuteur*.
Une **gare***	a station, a terminus.
Gare!*	(interjection) look out! get out of the way!
Gauche*	(*a*) left. Ex.: *Tournez à gauche*, turn to the left. *Il s'assit à ma gauche*, he sat on my left. (*b*) clumsy, awkward (of persons).

Une **gaule*** . . .	a long rod, a long stick.
La **Gaule*** . .	Gaul (the country).
Un **Gaulois*** . .	A Gaul.
Du **gaz*** . . .	gas.
De la **gaze*** . .	gauze (a kind of muslin).
Une **gelée*** . . .	(*a*) jelly. (*b*) frost.
Un **gendre*** . .	a son-in-law.
Gender . . .	*le genre.*
Un **gentilhomme*** .	a nobleman.
A **gentleman** . .	(in a general sense) *un monsieur.* (by education and manners) *un homme comme il faut.* A private gentleman (a man living upon his income), *un rentier.*
Un **geste*** . . .	a gesture.
A **jest** . . .	*une plaisanterie.*
Une **glace*** . . .	(*a*) ice. (*b*) looking-glass. (*c*) carriage-window.
Un **glas*** . . .	a knell.
Glass . . .	*du verre.* A pane of glass, *une vitre.* A pair of glasses, *des lunettes.*
Un **gland*** . . .	(*a*) an acorn. (*b*) a tassel.
A **gland** . . .	*une glande.*
La **glu*** . . .	birdlime.
Glue . . .	*de la colle forte.*

To go	(meaning to go away) *s'en aller, partir.* Ex.: At what time will you go? *à quelle heure vous en irez-vous* or *partirez-vous?*
Un **goëland***	a sea-gull.
Une **goëlette***	a schooner.
Good	(substantive) *bien, avantage.* (adjective) *bon.* (applied to a child) *sage.*
Un **gourmand***	a glutton.
Gourmander*	to reprove harshly.
Un **gourmet***	an epicure.
Une **gourmette***	a curb-chain (harness).
Un **goût***	a taste.
Goutte (fem.)*	(*a*) a drop. (*b*) gout. *Boire la goutte,* to take a drop (of spirit). *Boire une goutte,* to drink a drop (of anything). *Il n'y voit goutte,* he cannot see at all.
Un **gradin***	a tier, a bench (when the benches rise one above the other).
Un **gredin***	a scoundrel.
Granite	(notice the spelling) *du granit* (the *t* is sounded).

Une **grappe***	a bunch (of grapes).
A **grape**	*un grain de raisin.*
	A bunch of grapes, *une grappe de raisin.*

Une **gratification***	a gratuity.
A **gratification**	*une satisfaction, un plaisir.*

Gratifier*	to confer, to grant (a favour, a reward).
To **gratify**	*satisfaire, contenter, faire plaisir à.*

To **graze**	(to feed) *paitre, brouter.*
	(to touch lightly on the surface) *effleurer, raser, friser.*

Grêle*	(adjective) slim, thin (i.e. weak).
	(substantive) hail.
	Une grêle de coups, a shower of blows.

Grêlé*	(of crops, &c.) spoilt, destroyed (by hail).
	(of persons) pitted with the small pox.

Une **grève***	(*a*) a strand, beach, sand.
	(*b*) a strike (of workmen).
	Faire grève, to strike (to cease from work).
Grever*	to burden, to encumber (with debts, taxes, &c.).

Un **grief***	a grievance.
A **grief**	*un chagrin, une douleur.*

Une **griffe***	(a) a claw. (b) a stamped facsimile of a signature.
Un **gril***	a gridiron.
Une **grille***	(a) a grate. (b) a grating. (c) ornamental iron railing. (d) iron-rail gate.
Gris*	(a) grey. (b) intoxicated (familiar).
Se **griser***	to get intoxicated.
Ground	*la terre, le terrain, le sol.* (motive) *un sujet, un motif, une raison.* Back ground (of pictures), *le fond.*
Grounds	(dregs) *la lie, le sédiment.* (of coffee) *le marc (de café).* (of knowledge) *les principes.*
To **grow**	(to increase) *grandir, croître, pousser.* To grow old, *vieillir.* To grow less, smaller, *diminuer.*
A **guard**	(notice the spelling) *un garde.* A railway guard, *un chef de train.*
Un **guide***	(a) a guide. (b) a guide-book.
Une **guide***	a rein.

H

H. . . . . . Notice that in French the *h* whether mute or aspirated **so called** is never sounded.

The letter *h* is **said** to be aspirated in French when it prevents the elision of *e* or *a* in *le, la,* &c., preceding it. It is considered then as a consonant.

The following is a list of the more usual words in which the *h* is (so called) aspirated ([1]) : *La hache,* axe ; *un hachis,* mince meat, hash ; *hagard,* haggard; *la haie,* hedge; *le haillon,* rag, tatters ; *la haine,* hatred ; *haïr,* to hate ; *la halle,* market-place ; *une halte,* a halt ; *le hameau,* hamlet ; *la hanche,* hip ; *un hangar,* a cart-shed ; *la harangue,* harangue ; *hardi,* bold ; *un hareng,* a herring ; *le hasard,* hazard ; *la hâte,* haste; *haut,* high ; *hérisser,* to bristle ; *le héros,* hero ; (however in *héroïne, héroïque, héroïquement* and *héroïsme* the *h* is mute) ; *un hêtre,* a beech tree ; *le hibou,* owl ; *hideux,* hideous ; *la Hollande,* Holland ; *la honte,* shame ; *la houille,* coal ; *le houx,* holly-tree ; *une huée,* hooting ; *hurler,* to howl ; *une hutte,* a hut.

([1]) The word "aspirate" is evidently a misnomer when applied to the pronunciation of the letter *h* in French. We should suggest to substitute for the appellations *h* mute and *h* aspirated, those of *h* vowel and *h* consonant.

DICTIONARY OF DIFFICULTIES. 69

Un habit*	a coat.
A habit	(a custom) *une habitude.* A riding habit, *une amazone, un habit de cheval.*

Haggard	(notice the spelling) *hagard.*

Hair	*cheveux.* Ex.: *Il a les cheveux noirs.* (of animals) *poil.* Ex.: *Un chien à poil ras,* a short-haired dog. (of the mane and tail of horses, &c.) *crin* (mas.). (of a boar) *les soies* (fem.).
Une haire*	a hair shirt.

Halé*	towed.
Hâlé*	sunburnt, swarthy.
Hale	*robuste, vigoureux.*

Haleter*	to pant, to be out of breath, to gasp for breath.
To halt	(neuter verb) *faire halte.* (active verb) *faire faire halte à, arrêter.*

Half	(substantive) *la moitié.* Ex.: He has eaten half the cake, *il a mangé la moitié du gâteau.* (adjective) *demi.* (Demi placed before a noun is invariable, but agrees in gender when placed after. Ex.: *une demi-heure ; deux heures et demie.*) (adverb) *à demi, à moitié, presque.*

Une **halle*** . . .	market place (usually covered over).
A **hall** . . .	(entrance passage) *un vestibule*. (a manor-house) *un château*. (a large room) *une salle*. <small>The English word "hall" in the sense of a large room is sometimes used in French and is masculine.</small>
A **hammock** . .	(notice the spelling) *un hamac*.
A **hand** . . .	*une main*. (at cards) *un jeu*. (of a watch) *une aiguille*. (a workman) *un ouvrier*. I bought this book second-hand, *j'ai acheté ce livre d'occasion*. He is my right hand, *c'est mon bras droit*. To live from hand to mouth, *vivre au jour le jour*. To fight hand to hand, *se battre corps à corps*.
A **handle** . . .	(of a basket) *une anse*. (of a knife) *un manche*. (of a sword) *une poignée*. (of a broom) *un manche*. (of a wheelbarrow) *un bras*. (of a barrel organ) *une manivelle*. (of a frying pan) *une queue*.
Hardi* . . .	bold. Ex.: *Il est très hardi*, he is very bold.
Hardy . . .	*robuste, fort*. Ex.: He is hardy, *il est robuste*. (of plants) *vivace*.
Harvest . . .	(of corn) *la moisson*. (in a general sense) *la récolte*.

Hâve*	emaciated, wan.
Un **havre*** . .	a harbour.

Hazard . . . (notice the spelling) *le hasard*.
Par hasard, by chance.
Au hasard, at random, at a venture.
A tout hasard, at all hazards.

To **hear** . . . (a noise) *entendre*.
(news) *apprendre*, or *entendre dire*.
   Ex.: I heard he had enlisted, *j'ai entendu dire (or j'ai appris) qu'il s'était engagé*.
(of somebody) *entendre parler de*.
(from somebody) *avoir des nouvelles de*.
(a lesson) *faire réciter une leçon*.
Hear! hear! *bravo!* or *très bien !*

To **help** . . . *aider*.
(Notice the translation of sentences like the following):
I cannot help laughing, *je ne puis m'empêcher de rire*.

Hermit . . . (notice the spelling) *un ermite*.

Un **héraut*** . .	a herald.
Un **héros*** . .	a hero.

Une **herse*** . .	(*a*) harrow. (*b*) portcullis.
A **hearse** . .	*un corbillard, un char funèbre*.

Heure (fem.)*	hour, o'clock. *À la bonne heure!* that is right! Good! Well done! *De bonne heure,* early, soon. *Tout à l'heure,* by-and-by, presently, *or* just now, not long ago. *Le quart d'heure de Rabelais,* paying time, trying moment. *Un livre d'heures,* a prayer-book.
Heurter*	to knock against. *Heurter les préjugés de,* to shock the prejudices of.
To **hurt**	*faire mal à.*
Hisser*	to hoist, to haul up.
To **hiss**	*siffler.*
Homage	(notice the spelling) *un hom-mage.*
Honest	(notice the spelling) *honnête.* <small>*Honnête, honnêteté, honnêtement,* and *honneur* are spelt with **two n's** while *honorable, honorer, honoraire* have **one n** *only.*</small>
Hostage	(notice the spelling) *un otage.*
Hot	(over-spiced) *fort.* (see "*chaud.*")
Une **hotte***	a kind of basket carried on the back by means of straps.
Un **hôte***	(*a*) a host. (*b*) a guest.

Un **hôtel***	(*a*) an hotel. (*b*) a mansion. *L'hôtel de ville*, the town hall. *L'hôtel Dieu*, the principal hospital of a town. *L'hôtel des ventes*, auction rooms. *Un maître d'hôtel*, a proprietor of an hotel, *or* a house-steward.
Une **houe*** Du **houx***	a hoe. holly.
De la **houille*** La **houle*** De l'**huile***	coal (geology). the rolling, the swell (of the sea). oil.
House	(a dwelling) *une maison*. (at a theatre) *la salle*. (of parliament) *la chambre*. the House of Lords, *la chambre des pairs*. the House of Commons, *la chambre des communes*.
Housse* **Houssine***	(*a*) saddle-cloth. (*b*) furniture cover. a switch (a flexible twig).
Humer* To **hum**	to inhale. (of persons) *fredonner*. (of bees) *bourdonner*.
Hurler* To **hurl**	to howl, to roar. *jeter, lancer, précipiter*.

Un **hymne***.	(*a*) a warlike song. (*b*) a poem in honour of the gods.
Une **hymne***	a hymn sung in churches.

I

Un **idiome***	a dialect.
An **idiom**	*un idiotisme.*
Idle	(of questions, speeches, &c.) *oiseux* (fem. *oiseuse*). Ex.: *Des paroles oiseuses.* (in other cases) *oisif* (fem. *oisive*). Ex.: *Un homme oisif, une vie oisive.*
Ignorer*	not to know.
To **ignore**	*mépriser, dédaigner, ne pas tenir compte.* (jurisprudence) *déclarer qu'il n'y a pas lieu à poursuite.*
Les **impositions** (fem.)*	the taxes (*impôt* is more often used).
An **imposition**	(deceit) *une imposture, une supercherie.* (exaction) *une extorsion, un vol.* (at school) *un pensum* (pronounce *pin-somm*).
To **improve**	(in appearance) *embellir.* (in knowledge) *faire des progrès.* (on acquaintance) *gagner à être connu.* (morally) *devenir meilleur.* (wine) *s'améliorer, se bonifier.* To improve on anything, *perfectionner quelque chose.*

Incessamment* . .	(a) by-and-by, almost immediately. (b) incessantly.
Inconvenant* . .	improper, indecorous, unseemly.
Inconvenient . .	*incommode, pas commode, gênant.*
Un **inconvénient*** .	an inconvenience.
Indefatigable . .	(notice the spelling) *infatigable.*
Independent . .	(notice the spelling) *indépendant.*
Ingénu* . . .	candid, simple, childish.
Ingénieux* . .	ingenious.
Ingénuité (fem.)* .	candour, simplicity.
Ingenuity . .	*habileté, talent.*
Inhabité* . . .	uninhabited.
Inhabited . .	*habité.*
Injurier* . . .	to abuse, to insult.
To **injure** . .	*nuire à, faire tort à.*
Insensé* . . .	(substantive) (a) an unwise person. (b) a lunatic. (adjective) foolish, senseless.
Incensed . .	*exaspéré, furieux.*
Instamment* . .	urgently, earnestly. Ex.: *Il m'a prié instamment de le faire*, he earnestly asked me (he entreated me) to do it.
Instantanément* .	instantaneously.

Des instances*	entreaties. Ex.: *Faire de vives instances*, to entreat earnestly.
An **instance**	*un exemple.* For instance, *par exemple.*
Intelligence	(intellect) *l'intelligence* (fem.). (news) *une nouvelle, des nouvelles.* (information) *des renseignements.*
An **interval**	(notice the spelling) *un intervalle.*
Introduire*	to show in, to bring in.
S'introduire*	to gain admittance.
To **introduce**	(persons to one another) *présenter quelqu'un.* Ex.: Allow me to introduce to you Mr. So-and-so, *Permettez-moi de vous présenter Monsieur Un tel.*
Un **invalide***	(military) a pensioner.
An **invalid**	*un malade.*
To **invest**	(with power) *revêtir.* (a military term) *investir.* (money) *placer.*

J

Jacques*	James.
Jack	*Jean.*
Jalousie*	(*a*) jealousy. (*b*) Venetian blind.

Jeune* . . .	young.
Jeûne* . . .	fasting.
Joli*	pretty.
Jolly. . . .	*gai, joyeux.*
Jouer à* . . .	to play at (a game).
Jouer de* . .	to play on (an instrument).
	Jouer de malheur, to be unlucky, unfortunate, to have a run of ill-luck.
	Jouer des jambes, to take to one's heels.
Se **jouer*** . .	(*de quelqu'un*) to make game of (somebody).
	(*d'une difficulté*), to make light of a difficulty).
	(*de la mort*) to be fearless of death, to baffle death.
Jour*	(*a*) day (twenty four hours).
	(*b*) daylight.
	Au grand jour, in broad daylight.
	Voir le jour (elegant prose), to be born.
	Mettre à jour, to bring up to date (accounts).
	Vivre au jour le jour, to live from hand to mouth.
	Se faire jour au travers de (or *à travers*) *la foule,* to make one's way through the crowd.
Une **journée*** .	(*a*) day (from sunrise to sunset).
	(*b*) a day's work.
A **journey** . .	*un voyage.*
A **judge** . . .	(notice the spelling) *un juge.*
A **judgment** . .	(notice the spelling) *un jugement.*

K

To **kick** . . . (of persons) *donner des coups de pied.*
(of horses) *ruer.*

A **kite** . . . (a bird of prey) *un milan.*
(a toy) *un cerf-volant.*

To **know** . . . (implying study, or meaning to guess, to imagine, to be aware of, to understand) *savoir.* Ex.: I know my lesson, *je sais ma leçon.*—If you try to borrow money from him I know (*i.e., I can imagine*) what he will say, *si vous essayez de lui emprunter de l'argent je sais ce qu'il vous répondra.*—I know (*i.e., I guess*) what you mean, *je sais ce que vous voulez dire.*—Do you know (*i.e., are you aware*) that he has refused to come? *Savez-vous qu'il a refusé de venir.*
(In all other cases) *connaître.* Ex.: Do you know that man? *Connaissez-vous cet homme.*
(Notice: *Je sais cette chanson,* I know that song, *i.e.,* I have learned it, I can sing it.—*Je connais cette chanson,* I know that song, *i.e.,* I have heard it, I am aware of its existence.)
Know thyself, *connais-toi, toi-même.*

L

Un **labeur***.	toil, hard work.
Un **labour***	tillage, ploughing.
Labour	*le travail.*

Labourer*	to plough.
To **labour**	*travailler.*

Un **laboureur***	a ploughman.
A **labourer**	*un ouvrier.*

A bricklayer's labourer, *un manœuvre.*

Lâche* . . . (substantive) a coward.
(adjective) (*a*) cowardly.
(*b*) slack, loose. Ex.: *Ce nœud est trop lâche,* this knot is too loose.

Lâcher* . . . (*a*) to loosen.
(*b*) to let go.
Lâcher prise, to let go one's hold.
Lâcher pied, to retreat, to bolt.

Laid*	ugly.
Laie*	wild sow.
Lait*	milk.

Du petit lait, whey.
Un lait de poule, the yoke of an egg beaten with warm water and sugar, generally for invalids.
Un frère de lait, a foster-brother.
Un cochon de lait, a sucking pig.

Laisser*	to leave (active verb).
Lasser*	to tire.

Une **lame***	(*a*) a blade (of a knife, see "blade").
	(*b*) a wave, a billow.
Lame	*boiteux*.

Lande*	waste land, fen, moor.
Land	*la terre*.

A **language**	(notice the spelling) *un langage*.

Du **lard***	some bacon.
Some **lard**	*du saindoux*.

Large* (French)	wide, broad. Ex.: *Cette rivière est large*, this river is broad.
Large (English)	*grand*.
	(bulky) *gros*. Ex.: A large parcel, *un gros paquet*.
	(of fruit) *gros*. Ex.: A large apple, *une grosse pomme*.
	As large as life, *de grandeur naturelle*.

Une **largeur***	breadth.
Une **largesse***	largess, bounty.

Late (adjective)	(in the day) *avancé*. Ex.: He came at a late hour, *il est venu à une heure avancée*.
	(dead) *défunt, feu* (see "*feu*").
	(recent) *dernier*. Ex.: The late war, *la dernière guerre*.
	Of late years, *ces dernières années*.

DICTIONARY OF DIFFICULTIES.   81

Late (adverb)	*tard.* Ex.: He comes home late, *il rentre tard.*
	To be late (behind one's time), *être en retard.*
	Of late, *dernièrement, récemment.*
	It is getting late, *il se fait tard.*
To **lay**	(to put) *placer, mettre, poser.*
	(a bet) *faire (un pari).*
	(eggs) *pondre (des œufs).*
	(a snare) *dresser,* or *tendre (un piège).*
	(the cloth) *mettre (la nappe).*
	(the dust) *abattre (la poussière).*
	To lay down arms, *mettre bas* (or *déposer*) *les armes.*
	To lay down a principle, *poser un principe.*
A **leaf**	(of a tree) *une feuille.*
	(of a book) *une feuille, un feuillet.*
	(of a table) *une rallonge.*
Une **lecture***	a reading.
A **lecture**	(a discourse) *une conférence,*
	(a reprimand) *une semonce, une réprimande,* (familiarly *un savon*).
A **leg**	*jambe.*
	(of birds, insects, and small quadrupeds) *une patte.*
	(of cooked poultry) *une cuisse.*
	(of mutton) *un gigot.*
	(of tables) *un pied.*
	(of high boots) *une tige.*
Un **legs***	(pronounce *un lai*) legacy, bequest.

F

Lent*	slow.
Lent . . .	le carême.

A **lesson** . . .	(notice the spelling) *une leçon.*

Du **lest*** . . .	ballast (*see* " ballast ").
Leste* . . .	(*a*) nimble. (*b*) "free" (*i.e.* improper).

Un **lézard*** . . .	a lizard.
Une **lézarde*** . .	crevice, crack (in a wall).

Une **librairie*** . .	a bookseller's shop.
A **library** . . .	*une bibliothèque.*

La **lie***	dregs, grounds. *La lie du peuple*, the scum of the people.
A **lie** . . .	*un mensonge.* To give the lie, *donner un démenti.*

To **like** . . .	*aimer.* <small>Notice the translation of sentences like the following:</small> How do you like this house? *comment trouvez-vous cette maison ?* Do as you like, *faites comme vous voudrez.* Come if you like, *venez si vous voulez.* I should like to go there, *je voudrais bien y aller.* Would you like to come with us? *voudriez-vous* (or *voulez-vous*) *venir avec nous ?*

Une **lime*** . . .	a file (a tool).
Lime . . .	*de la chaux.* (for catching birds) *de la glu.* (a tree) *un tilleul.* (a fruit) *un citron, un limon.*
Un **limon*** . . .	(*a*) a kind of lemon. (*b*) slime, marshy mud.
Literal . . .	(notice the spelling) *litt*é*ral.*
Literature . . .	(notice the spelling) *la l*i*tt*é*rature.*
To **live** . . .	(to exist) *vivre.* (to reside) *demeurer à, habiter, résider.* Ex.: He lives in London, *il demeure à Londres, il habite Londres.* To live on (fish, &c.), *vivre de (poisson, etc.).*
Un **livre*** . . .	a book.
Une **livre*** . . .	a pound (money and weight). *Une livre parisis, une livre tournois,* old French coins; the former was worth about one shilling, the latter about tenpence.
Un **logeur*** . . .	a lodging-house keeper (common).
A **lodger** . . .	*un locataire.*
Loque (fem.)* . . .	rag.
A **lock** . . .	(of a door, &c.) *une serrure.* A double lock, *une serrure à double tour.* (of hair) *une boucle, une mèche de cheveux.* (of a canal) *une écluse.*

Lottery . . .	(notice the spelling) *une loterie*.
Louer* . . .	(*a*) to hire, to rent. (*b*) to let out (apartments, &c.). (*c*) to praise. *Je n'ai qu'à me louer de sa conduite*, I am highly pleased with him.
Un **loup*** . . .	a wolf.
Une **loupe*** . .	(*a*) a magnifying glass. (*b*) a wen (a tumour).
Une **louve*** . .	a she-wolf.

M

Mad	(of persons) *fou*. (of dogs) *enragé*.
Madam . . .	(notice the spelling) *madam*e.
Un **magot*** . .	(*a*) a baboon. (*b*) an ugly person (familiar). (*c*) a grotesque figure made of china, &c. (*d*) a hoard of money, a hidden treasure (familiar).
A **maggot** . .	*une larve*. (in a fruit) *un ver*. (for bait) *un asticot*.
A **major** . . .	(of infantry) *un chef de bataillon*. (of cavalry) *un chef d'escadrons*. A major-general, *un général de brigade*. A drum-major, *un tambour-major*.

To **make** . . .	*faire*.
	(followed by an adjective) *rendre*. Ex.: That will make you ill, *cela vous rendra malade*.

Un **malaise*** . .	a slight indisposition.
Malaisé* . . .	not easy, difficult.

Malhonnête* . .	(a) dishonest.
	(b) impolite, rude (*see* "rude").

Un **manche*** . .	a handle (of a knife, &c.).
Une **manche*** . .	a sleeve.
	La Manche, the English Channel.

Un **manœuvre*** . .	(a) a mason's labourer.
	(b) an inferior workman.
Une **manœuvre*** .	manœuvre.

Marble . . .	(a kind of stone) *du marbre*.
	(a toy) *une bille*.

Un **marchand*** . .	a tradesman.
	Un marchand des quatre saisons, a costermonger.
	Un marchand forain, a hawker who sells his goods at fairs.
A **merchant** . .	*un négociant*.

Une **mare*** . . .	a pool, a pond.
A **mare** . . .	*une jument*.

Un **maréchal*** . .	a marshal.
	Un maréchal des logis, a sergeant (in the cavalry).
	Un maréchal ferrant, a farrier.

La **marée*** . . .	(*a*) the tide. (*b*) sea fish.

Un **marin*** . . .	a sailor. *Un marin d'eau douce*, a landlubber.
La **marine*** . .	the navy.
The **marines** . .	*infanterie de marine, soldats de la marine.*

Un **marmot*** . .	(familiar) a brat. *Croquer le marmot* (familiar) to be kept waiting for a long time.
Une **marmotte*** .	a marmot.
Marmotter* . .	to mutter, to mumble.

A **marriage** . .	(notice the spelling) *un mariage*.

To **marry** . . .	(to give in marriage) *marier*. Ex.: *Elle a marié ses deux filles.* (ceremony performed by the priest) *marier*. Ex.: *L'évêque les a mariés.* (to get married) *se marier*. Ex.: *Il s'est marié l'année dernière.* (to espouse) *épouser*. Ex.: *Il a épousé sa cousine.*

Un **martyr*** . .	a martyr. *Le commun des martyrs*, the common herd.
Un **martyre*** . .	a martyrdom.

Une **masure***	(*a*) a hovel. (*b*) a house in ruin.
A **measure**	*une mesure.*

Un **mât***	(pronounce *mâh*) a mast. *Un mât de Cocagne*, a greasy pole (at fairs).
Mat*	(pronounce *matt*) not bright, not polished, dull (of metals, &c.). *Echec et mat*, checkmate.
A **mat**	(of straw) *un paillasson.* (of rush) *une natte.* (under dishes) *un dessous de plat.*

Un **matin***	a morning.
Un **mâtin***	a mastiff.

Une **mécanique***	a machine, machinery, piece of machinery.
A **mechanic**	*un artisan, un ouvrier.*

Une **mèche***	(*a*) a wick. (*b*) a whip-lash. (*c*) a lock (of hair). *La mèche est éventée*, the plot is discovered, the game is up.

Melancholy	(notice the spelling) *la mélancolie.*

Un **ménage***	(*a*) a household. (*b*) housekeeping. *Entrer en ménage*, to begin housekeeping. *Faire bon ménage*, to live happily together. *Une femme de ménage*, a charwoman.

Un **manège*** . . a riding-school.
Il répéta ce manège plusieurs fois, he repeated this manœuvre several times.

Ménager* . . . to husband, to manage with economy.
Ménager quelqu'un, to take care not to offend some-one.
Ménagez-vous, take care of yourself.
Ménagez vos forces, spare your strength ; *ménagez votre cheval,* spare (do not overwork) your horse.
Vouloir ménager la chèvre et le chou, to wish to run with the hare, and hold with the hounds.

To **manage** . . (*a*) *conduire, gouverner, diriger.*
(*b*) (commerce) *gérer.*
How did you manage to be disengaged so early ? *Comment vous êtes-vous arrangé* (or *comment avez-vous fait*) *pour être libre si tôt ?*

Un **mémoire*** . . (*a*) a statement of account.
(*b*) a report.
(*c*) a scientific or literary treatise.

La **mémoire*** . . memory,
Il a une mémoire de lièvre, his head is like a sieve.

Mépris (mas.)* . . contempt, scorn.
Méprise (fem.)* . mistake, oversight.

La **mer*** . . .	the sea.
	Un loup de mer, a sea dog (an expert sailor).
Une **mère*** . .	a mother.
	Une belle-mère, a mother-in-law, *or* a step-mother.

Un **mercier*** . .	haberdasher.
A **mercer** . .	*un marchand de soieries*, or *un négociant en soieries*.

Un **merlan*** . .	a whiting (fish).
Un **merle*** . .	a blackbird.
Une **merluche*** .	cod, dried but not salted.

Un **mess*** . . .	(military) mess, officers' table.
Une **messe*** . .	a mass.

Mettre* . . .	to put.
Se **mettre à*** . .	(followed by a verb) to begin to, to set to. Ex.: *Il se met à travailler trop tard*, he begins to work too late.
	Se mettre à table, to sit down to meals.
	Se mettre bien (or *mal*), to dre with good (or bad) taste.

Une **meule*** . .	(*a*) grindstone.
	(*b*) stack, rick (of hay),
Une **meute*** . .	a pack of hounds.
Une **émeute*** . .	a riot.

Un **meurtrier***	. .	a murderer.
Une **meurtrière***	.	a loophole.
Meurtrir*	. .	to bruise.
To **murder**	. .	*assassiner.*

To **miss** . . . *manquer.*
(to omit) *sauter.* Ex.: You missed a line, *vous avez sauté une ligne.*
To miss fire, *rater.*

Notice the translation of sentences like the following:

They miss you, *vous leur manquez,* or *ils vous regrettent beaucoup.*

Un **mode***	. .	a mood (grammatical term).
La **mode***	. .	the fashion.

A **mole** . . . (an animal) *une taupe.*
(on the skin) *une marque de naissance, un grain de beauté, un signe.*
(of a port) *une jetée, un môle.*

Momentané*	. .	momentary.
Momentous	. .	*important.*

De la **monnaie*** . . small change. Ex.: *Donnez-moi la monnaie d'un franc,* give me change for a franc.
La Monnaie, the Mint.
Je lui ai rendu la monnaie de sa pièce, I gave him tit for tat.

Some **money** . . *de l'argent* (mas.).

Monter*	(*a*) to go up, to ascend. (*b*) to wind up (a clock, a watch). (*c*) to mount, to ride (a horse, &c.). (*d*) to set (a diamond, &c.).
Montrer*	to show.
Le **moral***	spirits. Ex.: *Le moral des troupes est excellent*, the troops are in excellent spirits.
La **morale***	morals, ethics. (of fables, &c.) moral.
Un **moule***	a mould.
Une **moule***	a mussel (a shell-fish).
Mourir*	to die.
Se **mourir***	to be dying.
Un **mousse***	a ship's apprentice, a cabin-boy.
La **mousse***	(*a*) moss. (*b*) froth. (*c*) lather.
A **mouse**	*une souris*.
A **mouth**	(of man) *une bouche*. (of carnivorous animals) *une gueule*. (of a river) *une embouchure*.
Un **mulet***	a mule.
Un **mulot***	a field-mouse.
Un **mur***	a wall.
Mûr*	(of fruit) ripe. (of linen, &c.) old, nearly worn out.
Une **mûre***	mulberry.

N

Une **nappe***	a table-cloth. *Une nappe d'eau,* a sheet of water.
Nap	(of hats, &c.) *le poil.* (sleep) *un somme.* An afternoon nap, *une sieste.*

Une **natte*** . . . (a) (straw, cocoa-nut, indian) matting.
(b) plait of hair.

Un **navet*** . . . a turnip.
Une **navette*** . . a shuttle.

A **neck** . . . (of men and animals) *un cou.*
(of bottles) *un goulot.*
(of land) *une langue (de terre).*
To have a stiff neck, *avoir le torticolis.*

Nerveux* . . . (a) sinewy, wiry, muscular. Ex.: *Il a les bras nerveux,* his arms are sinewy.
(b) irritable, hysterical.

To be **nervous** . (to be shy) *être timide, être intimidé, être troublé.* — Ex.: She was so nervous that she could not speak, *elle était si troublée (si intimidée) qu'elle ne pouvait parler.*
(to be afraid) *être peureux, avoir peur.* Ex.: She is too nervous to remain alone, *elle est trop peureuse pour rester seule.*

Nice	(to the taste) *bon*. (pretty) *joli*. (amiable) *gentil*.
Noise* . . .	quarrel. Used only in *chercher noise à quelqu'un*, to pick a quarrel with somebody.
Noise . . .	*bruit*. (uproar) *un vacarme, un tapage, un fracas*.
A **nose** . . .	(of animals) *un museau*. (of persons) *un nez*. A flat nose, *un nez camus, un nez camard*. A turned-up nose, *un nez retroussé*.
To **nourish** . .	(notice the spelling) *nou**rr**ir*.
Now	(adverb) *maintenant, à présent, actuellement*. (of the past) *alors*. Ex.: He was now in great difficulty, *il était alors dans un grand embarras*. Just now, *tout à l'heure, à l'instant*. Now and then, *de temps en temps*. (conjunction) *or*. Ex.: Now, it so happened that, *or, il arriva que*.
Un **noyé*** . . .	a drowned person.
Un **noyer*** . .	a walnut tree.

Number	(expressing the order in which persons or things are placed) *un numéro*. Ex.: At the examination my number is five, *à l'examen j'ai le numéro cinq*.—I live No. 4, *je demeure au numéro 4*. (a quantity) *un nombre*. Ex.: They came in great numbers, *ils vinrent en grand nombre*.
A nurse	(a wet nurse) *une nourrice*. (for children) *une bonne (d'enfant)*. (for the sick) *une garde-malade*.

O

An object	(a thing) *un objet*. (aim, purpose, design) *un but*. (a grammatical word) *un complément, un régime*.
To observe	(to notice) *observer, remarquer*. (to point out) *faire observer, faire remarquer*.
Odd	(of numbers) *impair*. (strange) *étrange, singulier*. (droll) *drôle, original*. (only one of a pair) *déparié*. (of books) *dépareillé*.
An offence	(notice the spelling) *une offense*. To take offence, *s'offenser, se formaliser*. To give offence, *offenser, choquer*.

Un **office***	employment, functions. *L'office divin*, divine service.
Une **office***	a pantry.

Une **ombre***	shade *or* shadow.
Ombrage*	shade of trees. Ex.: *un ombrage impénétrable aux rayons du soleil.*
Ombreux*	shady (of forests).
Ombrageux*	(of persons) of a suspicious, distrustful nature. (of horses) shy, skitish.

Une **ombrelle***	a sunshade.
An **umbrella**	*un parapluie.* An umbrella case, *un fourreau de parapluie.*

Open	*ouvert.* Wide open, *grand ouvert.* Open-hearted, *franc.* In the open air, *en plein air.* In the open sea, *en pleine mer.* An open carriage, *une voiture découverte.*

An **order**	(a command) *un ordre.* (for goods) *une commande.* (for the theatre) *un billet de faveur.* To give an order (to command), *donner un ordre.* To give an order (for goods), *faire une commande.* Made to order (of clothes, &c.), *fait sur commande.*

An **order** (*continued*)	Until further orders, *jusqu'à nouvel ordre*. To put out of order (books, &c.), *déranger, mettre en désordre*. To put out of order (machines, clocks, &c.), *détraquer*.
Une **ordonnance***	(milit.) an orderly. (med.) a prescription.
Ornament	(notice the spelling) *un ornement*.

P

A **pack**	(of cards) *un jeu*. (of hounds) *une meute*.
Un **page*** Une **page***	a page (a boy). a page (of a book).
Du **pain*** Un **pain***	some bread. a loaf. *Un petit pain*, a roll. *Du pain frais, du pain tendre*, new bread. *Du pain rassis*, stale bread. *Du pain d'épices*, gingerbread. *Pain rôti*, toast.
A **pain**	*une douleur*. To give any one pain (mental), *faire de la peine à quelqu'un*. To give any one pain (physical), *faire mal à quelqu'un*.

To **paint** . . .	(notice the spelling) *peindre*.
A **painter** . . .	(notice the spelling) *peintre*.
Un **palais*** . .	(*a*) a palace. (*b*) a palate (of the mouth). *Le Palais de justice*, the law courts.
A **palisade** . .	(notice the spelling) *une palissade*.
Panser* . .	(*a*) to dress (wounds). (*b*) to groom (horses).
Penser à* . .	to think of.
Un **parallèle*** .	a parallel (a comparison).
Une **parallèle***.	a parallel (geometry).
Une **parcelle*** .	a particle.
A **parcel** . .	*un paquet*.
Pardonable .	(notice the spelling) *pardonnable*.
Des **parents*** .	relatives, relations. *Un proche parent*, a near relative.
Parents . .	*père et mère*.
Parer* . .	(*a*) to adorn. (*b*) to parry, to ward off.
Parier* . .	to bet. *Il y a dix à parier contre un*, it is ten to one that.
The **Parliament** .	(notice the spelling) *le parlement*.

Un **parti***	(*a*) a party (political). Ex.: *Un chef de parti*, a leader of a party. (*b*) part. Ex.: *Prendre le parti de quelqu'un*, to take any one's part. (*c*) resolution. Ex.: *J'ai pris mon parti*, I have formed my resolution, I have made up my mind. (*d*) match (marriage). Ex.: *Il a épousé un bon parti*, he has made a good match. *Tirer parti de tout*, to turn everything to account. *J'en ai tiré le meilleur parti possible*, I made the best of it.
Une **partie***	(*a*) part (of a whole). Ex.: *Il m'a rendu une partie de l'argent*. (*b*) a game (of cards, &c.). Ex.: *Voulez-vous faire une partie de cartes ?* Will you have a game at cards ? (*c*) a line (of business). *Une partie nulle*, a drawn game. *Une partie de plaisir*, a pleasure party.

Partial	(inclined to favour one party more than the other) *partial*. Ex.: *Un juge ne doit pas être partial*. (in all other meanings) *partiel*. Ex.: *Une éclipse partielle. Une somme partielle.*

A **partition** . . .	(music) *une partition.* (of planks, laths, &c.) *une cloison.* A partition wall, *un mur de refend.*
Participle . . .	(notice the spelling) *le partic***pe**.
A **partner** . . .	(commerce) *un associé.* (at a dance) *un danseur, un cavalier, un partenaire.* (at cards) *un partenaire.* A sleeping partner, *un commanditaire.*
A **passenger** . .	(on a boat) *un passager.* (on a railway) *un voyageur.*
Passer* . . .	to pass. *Il faut en passer par là,* we must submit to it, we must put up with it. *Il ne lui passe rien,* he does not overlook any of his faults. *Il a été passé par les armes,* He was shot (military execution). *Cela me passe!* It is beyond my comprehension.
Se **passer*** . .	(*a*) to happen. Ex.: *Cet évènement se passa il y a dix ans,* that event happened ten years ago. (*b*) to do without. Ex.: *Il ne peut se passer de vous,* he cannot do without you.

Une **patente***	. .	a tax paid for the exercise of a trade.
A **patent** .	. .	*un brevet.*

Un **patin***	. .	a skate.
Une **patine***	. .	patina (the very fine green rust which covers old bronze, etc.).

Un **patient***	. .	(*a*) a culprit about to be executed. (*b*) a patient undergoing a surgical operation.
A **patient**	. .	*un malade.*

Un **patron*** .	. .	(*a*) a patron saint. (*b*) an employer, a master. (*c*) a pattern (to be used as a model).
A **patron** .	. .	(a protector) *un protecteur.*

Une **paupière***	. .	an eyelid.
A **pauper**	. .	*un pauvre, un indigent.*

Un **pavillon***	. .	(*a*) a pavilion. (*b*) a flag (navy). *Amener son pavillon,* to strike her flag (of a ship). *Hisser le pavillon,* to hoist the flag. *Il a dû baisser pavillon,* he was compelled to yield, to give in.

To **pay**	(a bill, &c.) *payer une facture* (see "bill"). To pay for something, *payer quelque chose* (not *pour quelque chose*). Ex.: *J'ai payé mon chapeau.* To pay a visit, *faire* (or *rendre*) *une visite.* To pay a compliment, *faire un compliment.* To pay attention, *faire attention.* To pay back (money), *rendre, rembourser.* To pay out (to revenge one's self), *rendre la pareille.*
A **peasant**	(notice the spelling) *un paysan.*
Pêche (fem.)*	(*a*) angling, fishing. (*b*) a peach.
Un **péché***	a sin.
Pêcher*	to fish, to angle.
Pécher*	to sin. *Ce n'est pas par là qu'il pèche,* that is not his failing.
Un **pendule***	a pendulum.
Une **pendule***	a clock.
Une **pension***	(*a*) a pension. (*b*) board (food). Ex.: *Prendre quelqu'un en pension,* to receive some-one as a boarder. (*c*) a boarding-school. Ex.: *Il a mis son fils en pension,* he has sent his son to a boarding-school. *Une pension bourgeoise,* a family boarding-house. *Une pension viagère,* a life-annuity.

Un **percepteur***	a tax-collector.
Un **précepteur***	a preceptor, a private tutor.
Une **perle***	(a) a pearl. (b) a bead (of necklaces).
Personal	(notice the spelling) *perso*nn*el*.
A **pheasant**	(notice the spelling) *un* f*aisa*n.
Un **photographe***	a photographer.
Une **photographie***	a photograph.
Un **physicien***	a natural philosopher.
A **physician**	*un médecin*.
La **physique***	natural philosophy.
Some **physic**	*une médecine, un remède*.
Un **pic***	(a) a peak (mountain). (b) a pick axe. (c) a woodpecker. *A pic*, perpendicularly, steep.
To **pick**	(to gather) *cueillir*. (to choose) *choisir*. (a bone) *ronger (un os)*. (a quarrel) *chercher (querelle)*. (a lock) *crocheter (une serrure)*. (one's teeth) *se curer (les dents)*. To pick up, *ramasser*. Picked men, *des hommes d'élite*.
Une **pie***	a magpie. *Il croit avoir trouvé la pie au nid*, he has found a mare's nest. *Un cheval pie*, a piebald horse.
A **pie**	(of meat) *un pâté*. (of fruit) *une tourte*.

Une **pièce***	(a) a room, an apartment.
	(b) a patch.
	Une pièce de vin, a cask of wine.
	Une pièce de théâtre, a play.
A **piece**	(a fraction, a small piece), *un morceau*. Ex.: A piece of bread, *un morceau de pain*.
Piler*	to pound, to crush.
Piller*	to pillage, to plunder.
To **pile**	*entasser, empiler*.
	To pile arms, *former les faisceaux*.
Pink	(flower) *un œillet*.
	(colour) *rose*.
A **pipe**	(for smoking) *une pipe*.
	(a tube) *un conduit, un tuyau*.
	a bag-pipe, *une cornemuse, une musette*.
Une **pique***	a pike (a weapon).
Un **pique***	spades (cards).
A **pike**	(fish) *un brochet*.
Piquer*	to prick, to sting.
	Piquer un soleil (fem.), to blush.
	Piquer une tête, to take a header, to fall head foremost.
	Piquer des deux, to spur one's horse to the quick, to start at full gallop.
	Piquer la curiosité, to excite curiosity.
Se **piquer de***	(a) to pride oneself in.
	(b) to be offended. Ex.: *Il se pique d'un rien*, a trifle offends him.
A **pit**	(a hole in the ground) *une fosse*.
	(at the theatre) *le parterre*.

Pity	*la pitié.* It is a pity, *c'est dommage.* It is a great pity, *c'est bien* (or *grand*) *dommage.*
Un **placard***	(*a*) placard. (*b*) a cupboard (in a wall).
Une **place***	(*a*) room, a seat. Ex.: *Vous avez pris ma place,* you have taken my seat. *Faites-lui place,* make room for him. (*b*) a square (an open space at the junction of several streets). (*c*) a stronghold (a military term). Ex.: *La place se rendit* (see "*se rendre*") *au bout de huit jours.* (*d*) employment. Ex.: *Il est sans place,* he is out of employment. *Il ne peut demeurer en place,* he cannot stand still.
Plaindre* Se **plaindre***	to pity. to complain. *J'ai bien lieu de me plaindre,* I have good reason to complain.
Plat (adj.)*** Un **plat*** A **plate**	flat. a dish. *une assiette.*
A **plot**	(a stratagem) *un stratagème.* (a conspiracy) *une conspiration, un complot.* (of a comedy) *une intrigue.* (of ground) *une petite pièce de terre.*

Une **plume***	(*a*) a feather.
	(*b*) a pen, a nib.
A plum	*une prune.*

Plus tôt*	sooner, earlier.
Plutôt*	rather.

Un **poêle***	(*a*) a stove.
	(*b*) a pall.
Une **poêle***	a frying-pan.

Un **poids***	a weight.
Un **pois***	a pea.

Une **poignée***	(*a*) a handful.
	(*b*) a hilt (of swords).
Le **poignet***	the wrist.

Un **poing***	a fist.
Un **point***	(*a*) a dot.
	(*b*) a full stop.
	(*c*) a stitch (of needlework).
	(*d*) a stitch (a pain in the side).
Une **pointe***	a point (a sharp end).
	Marcher sur la pointe du pied, to walk on tiptoe.

Un **poison***	a poison.
Un **poisson***	a fish.
	Un poisson d'avril, an April fool.

A pole	(geography) *un pôle.*
	(a long staff), *une perche.*
	(of a carriage) *un timon.*
	A greasy pole (at fairs), *un mât de cocagne.*
	(a native of Poland) *un Polonais.*

Poli*	(a) polite.
	(b) polished. Ex.: *De l'acier poli*, polished steel.
Une **pomme de pin***.	a fir cone.
A **pine-apple** .	*un ananas*.
Le **port***	(a) harbour, port.
	(b) postage (of letters).
	(c) carriage (of parcels).
Une **portière***	(a) a carriage door.
	(b) a thick curtain before a door.
	(c) feminine of *portier* (doorkeeper).
Un **poste***	(a) post. Ex.: *Il est à son poste*, he is at his post.
	(b) a police station. Ex.: *On conduisit l'ivrogne au poste.*
	(c) a guardhouse.
La **poste***	post-office.
Un **pouce***	(a) a thumb.
	(b) an inch.
Une **poupée***	a doll.
Un **poupon***	a baby, a chubby faced baby.
Pousser*	(a) to push.
	(b) to grow, to shoot forth (of plants).
	(c) to utter (a cry). *Pousser un cri.*
	(d) to heave (a sigh). *Pousser un soupir.*

Un pré*	a meadow.
Près*	near.
Un prêt*	a loan.
Prêt*	(adjective) ready, willing. Ex.: *Il est prêt à mourir*, he is ready (or willing) to die.

Au premier*	on the first floor. Ex.: *Il demeure au premier*.
En première*	in a first class railway carriage.

Presbyte*	far sighted (short sighted is *myope*).
Un Presbytère*	a vicarage, a parsonage.
Presbytérien*	Presbyterian.

Présentement*	at present, now.
Presently	*tout à l'heure, bientôt, sous peu.*

Prêter*	(*a*) to lend. (*b*) to stretch, to give (of leather, &c.). *Prêter serment*, to take oath. *Prêter le flanc à*, to lay one's self open to (reproaches, accusations, &c.).

Prévenir*	(*a*) to anticipate and prevent. Ex.: *Prévenir un accident*. (*b*) to inform. Ex.: *Je l'ai prévenu de votre arrivée*. (*c*) to warn. *Un prévenu*, a prisoner before trial.
To prevent	*empêcher.*

Une prévention*	prejudice, bias.
A prevention	*un empêchement, un obstacle.*

Priser*	(a) to take snuff. (b) to prize, to value. *Un commissaire priseur,* an appraiser, an auctioneer.
Prisoner	(notice the spelling) *un prison-**nier**.*
Un **procès***	a lawsuit.
Process	(gradual progress), *le cours, la marche.* (method, arrangement), *le procédé.*
Un **prodige***	a prodigy.
Prodigue*	prodigal.
Prominent	(notice the spelling) *pro**é**minent.*
Propre*	(a) proper, correct. Ex.: *Le mot propre.* (b) (placed before a noun) own. Ex.: *Mon propre fils,* my own son. (c) (placed after a noun) clean. Ex.: *Des mains propres,* clean hands. However, *en main propre* means "in one's own hands." *Il est propre à tout,* he is fit for anything.
La **propreté***	cleanliness.
Propriété (fem.)*	property.
Propriety	*les convenances, la bienséance.*
Une **prune***	a plum. (Soldiers' slang), a bullet, a shot.
A **prune**	*un pruneau, une prune sèche.*

Punch	(of the puppet show) *Polichinelle* (mas.).
	(a beverage) *du punch* (pronounce ponh-sh).
	(an instrument) *un emportepièce.*

Pupille* . . .	(*a*) ward (a minor under the care of a guardian).
	(*b*) a pupil of the eye.
A pupil . . .	(a scholar) *un élève.*

Q

A quarrel . . .	(notice the spelling) *une qu**er**elle.*
	To settle a quarrel (by fighting), *vider une querelle.*
	To settle a quarrel (by explanation), *s'expliquer.*
Que*	(*a*) as. Ex.: *Il est aussi instruit* **que** *son frère.*
	(*b*) because. Ex.: *Si je ne suis pas allé chez vous c'est* **que** *j'étais malade.*
	(*c*) before. Ex.: *Je ne partirai point* **que** *je ne vous ai vu.*
	(*d*) how! Ex.: **Que** *c'est difficile.*
	(*e*) how much, how many! Ex.: **Que** *d'argent il a dépensé !*
	(*f*) if. Ex.: *Si vous lui écrivez et* **qu'***il vous réponde.*
	(*g*) in order that. Ex.: *Approchez* **que** *je vous entende.*
	(*h*) let! Ex.: **Qu'***il entre !*
	(*i*) only. Ex.: *Nous n'avons écrit* **que** *deux lettres.*

Que* (*continued*)	(*j*) since. Ex.: *Il y a dix ans* **que** *je ne l'ai vu.*
	(*k*) than. Ex.: *Vous êtes plus grand* **que** *moi de trois centimètres.*
	(*l*) that. Ex.: *Il m'a dit* **que** *vous le saviez.*
	(*m*) till. Ex.: *Attendez* **qu'**il *vous réponde.*
	(*n*) unless. Ex.: *Ils ne boivent jamais* **qu'**ils *n'aient soif.*
	(*o*) what? Ex.: **Que** *faites vous?*
	(*p*) when. Ex.: *A peine eut-il lu votre lettre* **qu'**il *s'en alla.*
	(*q*) whether. Ex.: **Qu'**il *pleuve ou non je sortirai.*
	(*r*) whom. Ex.: *Le monsieur* **que** *nous avons vu.*
	(*s*) why? Ex.: **Que** *ne le disiez-vous plus tôt?*
	(*t*) without. Ex.: *Il ne sort jamais* **qu'**il *ne s'enrhume.*
	(*u*) yet. Ex.: *Il aurait tout ce qu'il demande* **qu'**il *ne serait pas satisfait.*
	Que ne puis-je vous aider! how I wish I could help you!
	Je n'ai que faire de vos conseils, I have no need of your advice.
Question*	to ask a question, *faire une question;* or, *poser une question* (**not** *demander une question*).
Une **quille***	(*a*) a skittle.
	(*b*) a keel (of a boat).
A **quill**	*une plume d'oie.*
	A quill driver, *un gratte-papier.*

Un **quiproquo*** . .	. a mistake, a misunderstanding.
Quid pro quo	. *un équivalent*.
Quoi que* . .	. whatever. Ex.: *Quoi que vous disiez*, whatever you may say.
Quoique* . .	. although. Ex.: *quoiqu'il soit pauvre*, although he be poor.

R

Raisonner* . .	. to reason.
Résonner* . .	. to resound.
Ralentir* . .	. to slacken (speed).
To **relent** . .	. *se radoucir, se laisser fléchir*.
Une **rame*** . .	. (*a*) an oar. (*b*) a ream (of paper).
Un **rameau*** . .	. a bough, a branch. *Le dimanche des rameaux*, Palm Sunday.
A **ram** . .	. (sheep) *un bélier*. (of a ship), *un éperon*. A battering ram, *un bélier*.
Rampant* . .	. (*a*) creeping, crawling, crouching. (*b*) (heraldic) rampant.
Rampant . .	. *prédominant, effréné, très répandu*.
A **rampart** . .	. (notice the spelling) *un rempart*.
Rassembler* . .	. to assemble, to collect.
Ressembler à* .	. to resemble.

Un **râtelier***	(*a*) a rack (in stables). (*b*) a rack (for rifles, &c.). (*c*) (obsolete) a set of teeth.
Un **rayon***	(*a*) a ray (of light, &c.). (*b*) a radius. (*c*) a spoke (of a wheel). (*d*) a shelf. (*e*) a department (in a shop). *Un rayon de miel*, a honey-comb.
Reasonable	(notice the spelling) *r*ai*so*nn*able*.
A **rebel**	(notice the spelling) *un rebelle*.
To **recommend**	(notice the spelling) *recommander*.
Recouvrer*	to recover, to regain. Ex.: *Il a recouvré la santé*.
Recouvrir*	to cover again.
Un **recteur***	the head of an academy.
A **rector**	*un curé*.
A **reflection**	(notice the spelling) *une réflexion*.
Un **régal***	(*a*) a feast, a treat (food). (*b*) an excellent or a favourite dish.
Regal	*royal*.
Un **regard***	a look.
Regard	*égard*, respect. With regard to, *quant à*. Out of regard for, *par égard pour*. Give him my kind regards, *dites-lui bien des choses de ma part*.

Une **règle***	(*a*) a rule. (*b*) a ruler (an instrument to draw lines).
Les **reins***	loins.
Reins	(straps of a bridle) *les rênes*.
Relier*	to bind (books).
To **rely**	*compter sur*.
Remettre*	(*a*) to put again, to put on again. (*b*) to put off, to delay.
Se **remettre***	(*a*) to compose one's self, to calm one's self. (*b*) to grow well again, to recover.
S'en **remettre à***	to refer to, to leave to (meaning to trust to). Ex.: *Il s'en remet à vous*, he refers it to you; *or*, he leaves it to you.
Rendre*	to give back.
Se **rendre***	(*a*) to surrender. Ex.: *Il se rendit sans coup férir*, he surrendered without striking a blow. (*b*) to go to, to repair to. Ex.: *Il se rendit à Paris*, he went to Paris.
Être **rendu***	(familiar). (*a*) to be tired out. (*b*) to have reached one's destination.

H

A **rent**	(of houses, apartments, &c.), *un loyer*.
	(of farms) *un fermage*.
	(in garments) *un accroc* (pronounce *accro*), *une déchirure*.
Une **rente***	(*a*) an income.
	(*b*) stock, funds, consols.
Un **rentier***	a gentleman living upon his income.

Un **repaire***	a lair, a haunt.
Un **repère***	(or *un point de repère*) a guiding mark, a land mark.
Repairs	*réparations*.
	In thorough repair, *en bon état*.
	Out of repair, *en mauvais état*.

Repartir*	(*a*) to start again, to set out again.
	(*b*) to reply, to retort.
Répartir*	to divide, to distribute.

Repasser*	(*a*) to pass again.
	(*b*) to call again (to visit again). Ex.: *Dites-lui que je repasserai demain*, tell him that I shall call again to-morrow.
	(*c*) to iron.
	Repassez votre leçon, look over your lesson again.

To **replace**	(to place again, to put back) *replacer*.
	(to take the place of) *remplacer*.
	Se faire remplacer, to get a substitute.

Reprendre* . . (*a*) to take again.
                     (*b*) to take back.
                     (*c*) to blame, to censure. Ex.: *Reprenez vos amis en secret.*
                     (*d*) to correct a mistake made in speaking. Ex.: *Il a dit un mot pour un autre, mais il s'est repris aussitôt.*
                     On ne m'y reprendra pas! (or *plus!*) (familiar) I shall not be caught at that again in a hurry!
                     Que je vous y reprenne! (threat) Let me catch you at it again!

Resonner* . . (pronounce "re-sonner") to ring again.

Résonner* . . (pronounce "ré-zonner" to resound.

Responsible . . (notice the spelling) *responsable.*

Resource . . (notice the spelling) *une ressource.*

Rest . . . (the remainder) *le reste.*
                     (repose) *le repos.*
                     (support) *un appui, un support.*
                     A crotchet-rest, *un soupir.*

To **rest**	(to repose) *se reposer.* (to sleep) *dormir.* (to doze), *sommeiller, être assoupi.* (to stop) *rester, s'arrêter.* (to lie down) *se coucher.* (to lean against) *s'appuyer, être appuyé.* (to be placed upon) *reposer sur, être placé sur.*
Rester*	to remain.
Résumer*	to sum up, to recapitulate. *Résumer un discours,* to give a summary of a speech.
To **resume**	*reprendre, continuer.*
Retourner*	to return, to go back.
Se **retourner***	to turn round, to look behind. *N'y retournez pas!* (*a*) do not go there again, (*b*) do not do it again or you will smart for it. *Je n'y retournerai pas.* (*a*) I will not go there again. (*b*) I will not do it again or " chance " it again.
To **return**	(to come back) *revenir.* Ex.: I shall start at one o'clock, and return at three, *je partirai à une heure, et je reviendrai à trois.* (to go back) *retourner.* (to give back) *rendre.* (to send something back) *renvoyer (quelque chose).*

Revenir* . . . (*a*) to come back.
(*b*) to amount to, to come to, Ex.: *Mon voyage m'est revenu à mille francs*, my journey came to £40. *Les deux choses reviennent au même*, the two things amount to (come to, are tantamount to) the same.
(*c*) to remember (familiar). Ex.: *Son nom ne me revient pas*, I cannot remember his name.
(*d*) to please (familiar). Ex.: *Cet homme ne me revient pas*, that man does not please me (*i.e.*, I do not like his look).
(*e*) to get over (an astonishment). Ex.: *Je n'en reviens pas!* I cannot get over that!
Revenir à soi, to recover one's senses, to come to.

Revenir de loin* . (*a*) to come from a distant place.
(*b*) to recover from a severe illness.

Du rhum* . . . (pronounce "romm") some rum.
Un rhume* . . (pronounce "rümm") a cold.
Un rhume de cerveau, a cold in the head.
Un gros rhume, a violent cold.

Rheumatism . . (notice the spelling) *un rhumatisme.*

Une ride* . . . (*a*) a wrinkle.
(*b*) a ripple (on the water).

A ride . . . (on horseback) *une promenade* (or, *une course*) *à cheval.*
(in a carriage) *une promenade en voiture.*
(in a cab) *une course.*

To ride . . . *monter à cheval.* Ex.: Can you ride? *savez-vous monter à cheval?*
(for pleasure) *se promener à cheval.*
To ride to a place, *aller à cheval à.*
To ride (so many miles), *faire (tant de kilomètres) à cheval.*

Right . . . . (the right hand side) *la droite.* Ex.: He sat on my right, *il était assis à ma droite.*
The right side (of a cloth, &c.), *l'endroit.*
Have I a right to do it? *Ai-je le droit de le faire?*

To be **right** . . (of persons) *avoir raison.*
(of an account) *être juste, être exact, être bien le compte.*

A ring	un anneau. Ex.: *Il attacha la bride de son cheval à un anneau de fer scellé dans le mur.* (for the fingers) *une bague.* (a wedding-ring) *une alliance, une bague de mariage.* (in elegant prose) *un anneau nuptial.* (a circle) *un cercle, un rond.* Ex.: They formed a ring round him, *ils formèrent un cercle autour de lui.*
Rogue*	proud, haughty. Ex.: *Il m'a répondu d'un ton rogue.*
A rogue	*un coquin, un fripon.*
Un rôle*	a part, a character (theatre). *A tour de rôle,* in turn, by rotation.
A roll	(of paper, &c.) *un rouleau.* (a small loaf) *un petit pain.* (of a drum) *un roulement (de tambour).* To call the roll, *faire l'appel.*
Un roman*	a novel.
Roman	*romain.*
Romantic	(persons and adventures) *romanesque.* (scenerie) *romantique.*
A roof	(of a house) *un toit.* (of an omnibus) *une impériale.* (of the mouth) *le palais.*

A room	(in a general sense) *une pièce*. Ex.: A six-roomed flat, *un appartement de six pièces*. A bedroom, *une chambre à coucher*. A dining-room, *une salle à manger*. A drawing-room, *un salon*. There is room for three, *il y a de la place pour trois*. There is no room, *il n'y a pas de place*. Make room for him, *faites-lui place*.
Le **rose***	rose colour, pink.
Une **rose***	a rose (a flower). *Découvrir le pot aux roses* (familiar) to find out a secret.
Un **roseau***.	a reed.
La **rosée***	dew (*see* " dew ").
Une **roue***	a wheel.
Roux*	yellowish red. *La lune rousse*, April moon.
Une **rue***.	a street.
Rude*.	harsh, rough.
Rude	*grossier, malhonnête* (see "*malhonnête*").
Ruer*.	to kick (of horses, &c.).
Se **ruer sur***	to rush upon, to dash upon.

S

Sabbat*	(*a*) sabbath. (*b*) uproar, great noise. (*c*) nocturnal meeting of witches.

Du **sable***	some sand.
Sable	(a fur) *de la martre* (or *marte*), *de la zibeline*. (adjective) *noir, sombre, de deuil*.

Sale*	dirty.
Salé*	salted.
Salle*	(*a*) a hall. (*b*) house (theatre). Ex.: *La salle était pleine,* or *était comble,* there was a full house. (*c*) a ward (hospital). *Une salle à manger,* a dining-room. *Une salle d'armes,* a fencing school. *Une salle d'asile,* an infant school.
A **sale**	*une vente*.

Une **sangle***	a girth, a wide strap.
Un **sanglier***	a wild boar.

Un **sarment***	a vine branch, a vine shoot.
Un **serment***	an oath (a solemn promise).

Un **saut***	a leap, a jump.
Un **sceau***	a seal (a stamp).
Un **seau***	a pail, a bucket.

Se **sauver***	(a) to save one's self. (b) to run away.
A **scale**	(of drawings, maps, &c.) *une échelle*. (of a balance) *un plateau*. (of fish, snakes) *une écaille*.
A **seal**	(a stamp) *un cachet, un sceau*. (an animal) *un veau marin*.
Un **séminaire*** A **seminary**	a clerical college. *un pensionnat, une institution*.
Sensible* **Sensible**	sensitive. (judicious) *sensé*.
Une **sentence*** A **sentence**	a maxim. (grammar) *une phrase*. (law) *une sentence, un jugement, un arrêt*.
Sentir*	(a) to feel. (b) to smell.
Le **serein*** Un **serin***	evening dew. a canary bird.
Une **serre***	(a) a greenhouse, a conservatory (*see* "conservatoire"). (b) talon (of a bird of prey).

A **set**	(of earthenware) *un service.* (of precious stones) *une parure.* (of studs) *une garniture.*
A **shaft** . . .	(of mines) *un puits.* (of a cart) *un brancard.* (of a lance) *le bois.*
To **sharpen** . .	(a knife) *aiguiser, affiler.* (a pencil) *tailler.*
Shell	(of eggs and fruit) *une coque, une coquille.* (of oysters) *une coquille, une écaille.* (of a house) *la carcasse.* (a bomb) *un obus.*
A **shoe** . . .	(for horses) *un fer (à cheval).* (for persons) *un soulier.* a wooden shoe, *un sabot.*
To **shoot** . . .	(to bud) *pousser.* (with fire-arms) *tirer un coup de fusil, de pistolet, de canon,* &c. I shot at him, *je lui ai tiré un coup de fusil, de pistolet, etc.* I shot him, *je l'ai tué d'un coup de fusil, de pistolet, etc.* I shot him dead, *je l'ai tué raide.* I shot him in the leg, *je lui ai logé une balle dans la jambe,* or, *je l'ai atteint (or je l'ai blessé) d'un coup de fusil à la jambe.* (military execution) *fusiller.*

A shop	*un magasin.* Ex.: *Le magasin d'un bijoutier.* (where eatables, &c., are sold) *une boutique.* Ex.: *La boutique d'un boulanger, d'un épicier.* Linen-draper's shop, *magasin de nouveautés.* A tobacconist's shop, *un bureau de tabac,* or *un débit de tabac.*
Shy	(bashful) *timide.* (not fond of society) *sauvage.* (of horses) *ombrageux.* To shy (of horses) *faire un écart.*
Sick To **feel sick**	(ill) *malade.* (to be affected with nausea) *avoir mal au cœur.* To feel sick at heart, *avoir la mort dans l'âme.*
Siffler*	(*a*) to hiss. (*b*) to whistle.
Since	(because) *puisque.* Ex.: Since you like it, *puisque vous l'aimez.* (from such a time) *depuis.* Ex.: I have not seen him since you left, *je ne l'ai pas vu depuis votre départ.*

To **sink**	(in the mud) *enfoncer, s'enfoncer*. (of vessels) *couler à fond, couler bas, sombrer*. (of patients) *baisser, s'affaiblir*. (a well, a shaft) *percer, creuser*.
To **sit**	*s'asseoir*. (of courts, judges) *siéger*. (of birds, for hatching) *couver*. (for one's portrait) *poser*.
To **sit up**	(not to stoop) *se tenir droit*. (not to go to bed) *veiller*. To sit up all night, *passer la nuit*.
A **slice**	*une tranche*. (of bread and butter) *une tartine*.
A **sling**	(for a broken arm) *une écharpe*. To carry one's arm in a sling, *porter*, or *avoir le bras en écharpe*. (a weapon) *une fronde*.
Sobre* Sober	abstemious, temperate, frugal. (not intoxicated) *pas ivre*.
Le **solde*** La **solde***	balance of an account. a soldier's pay.
A **sole**	(a fish) *une sole*. (of the foot) *la plante des pieds*. (of shoes, boots) *une semelle*.
Solicitude	(notice the spelling) *la sollicitude*.

Un **solliciteur***	one who solicits.
A **solicitor**	(lawyer) *un avoué*.

Sombre*	dark, gloomy.
Sombrer*	to sink, to go down (ships).
Assombrir*	to darken.

Un **somme***	a short sleep, a nap. *Je n'ai fait qu'un somme toute la nuit.* I never woke up once all night.
Une **somme***	a sum. *Une bête de somme*, a beast of burden.

Sommeiller*	to doze, to slumber.
Un **sommelier***	(*a*) a butler. (*b*) a cellarman.

Son*	(*a*) his, her, its. (*b*) sound (noise). (*c*) bran.

Un **songe***	a dream.
A **song**	(of persons) *une chanson, un chant*. (of bird) *un chant*. (a trifle) *un rien, une bagatelle*.

Le **sort***	fate, lot. *Tirer au sort*, to draw lots. *Le sort en est jeté*, the die is cast.
La **sorte***	sort, kind.

Une **sottise***	a folly, a silly thing. *Dire des sottises à quelqu'un*, to abuse somebody (*see* "abuse").

Souffler*	(a) to blow. (b) to breathe. (c) to prompt (actors, &c.). (d) to huff (at draughts).
Un **soufflet***	(a) bellows. (b) a box on the ear. (c) an affront, a humiliation.
Un **sifflet***	a whistle.
Souiller*	to soil.
Un **soulier***	a shoe.
Un **souper***	a supper.
Un **soupir***	a sigh.
Un **souris***	a smile. (*Un sourire* is more often used).
Une **souris***	a mouse. *Une chauve-souris*, a bat (the animal).
To **spend**	(money) *dépenser*. (time) *passer*.
Spirituel*	(a) spiritual. (b) witty. Ex.: *Cet homme est très spirituel*, that man is very witty.
A **spout**	(of kitchen utensils) *un bec*. (of a house) *une gouttière*. (at sea) *une trombe*.
Spring	(a season) *le printemps*. (of water) *une source*. (of a watch, &c.) *un ressort*. (the main spring) *le grand ressort*. (a leap) *un saut*. To take a spring before jumping, *prendre son élan*.

A **squadron**	(of cavalry) *un escadron*. (of ships) *une escadre, une division*.
Staff	(military) *un état-major*. (of a school, &c.) *le personnel*, or *le corps enseignant*. (of a newspaper) *la rédaction*. (music) *la portée*. (a stick) *un bâton*.
To **stand**	(of persons) *se tenir droit, se tenir debout*. (of houses, &c.) *être situé, se trouver*.
Une **station***	(*a*) a station. (*b*) a cab stand.
Une **statue*** Un **statut***	a statue. a statute.
A **stone**	(a pebble) *une pierre*. (of grapes, pears, apples) *un pépin*. (of other fruit) *un noyau*. (a hailstone) *un grêlon*. To leave no stone unturned, *remuer ciel et terre*.
To **stoop**	(with old age) *se voûter*. (in order to pick up something) *se baisser*. (in a figurative sense) *s'abaisser, s'humilier*.

To **stop**	*arrêter.* Ex.: Stop him! *arrêtez-le!*
	(a steam-boat, &c.) *stopper.*
	(at a place) *rester.* Ex.: We shall stop a week in Paris, *nous resterons une semaine à Paris.*
	Stop! *arrêtez-vous!*
	Stop thief! *au voleur!*
	To stop up, *boucher.*
	To stop payment, *suspendre,* or *cesser les payements.*
	To stop any one from doing something, *empêcher quelqu'un de faire quelque chose.*
Un **store***	a roller-blind, a window-blind.
A **store**	*une provision.*
	In store, *en réserve.*
To **strike**	(to hit) *frapper.*
	(iron) *battre (le fer).*
	(of clocks) *sonner.*
	(to lower a ship's flag) *amener le pavillon d'un vaisseau,* or *baisser pavillon.*
	(to cease from work) *faire grève,* or *se mettre en grève.*
	To strike up, *commencer à jouer.*
	It strikes me that . . . *il me semble que* . . .
A **string**	*une ficelle.*
	(of shoes) *un lacet.*
	(of bonnet) *une bride.*
	(of a bow) *une corde.*
	(of a violin) *une corde.*

To **stuff**	(for preserving dead animals) *empailler*. (cookery) *farcir*. (furniture) *rembourrer*.
Subsistence	(notice the spelling) *une subsistance*.
To **suceeed**	(to come next) *succéder*. (to prosper) *réussir*.
A **suit**	(of cards) *une couleur*. (of clothes) *habillement complet*. (a petition) *une requête, une pétition*. To bring a suit (jurisprudence), *intenter un procès, une action, une poursuite*.
Suppléer*	to make up (for what is deficient). Ex.: *La valeur supplée au nombre*, valour makes up for the deficiency of number.
Supplier*	to beseech, to implore, to entreat.
To **supply**	*fournir*.
Supporter*	(*a*) to support. (*b*) to put up with, to bear. Ex.: *Je ne puis supporter ce bruit*, I cannot bear that noise.

Sur*	(preposition) *upon*. (adjective) *sour*.
Sûr*	*sure*.

Un **surnom***	a nickname.
A **surname**	*un nom de famille*.

To **sweep**	*balayer*. (a chimney) *ramoner*.

Syllable	(notice the spelling) *une syllabe*.

T

Une **tache***	a stain. *Une tache de rousseur*, a freckle.
Une **tâche***	a task.

La **taille***	(*a*) the size, the height (of persons and animals). (*b*) the waist (of persons). (*c*) the pruning of trees. *Frapper d'estoc et de taille*, to cut and thrust (fencing).
A **tail**	*une queue*.

A **tailor**	(notice the spelling) *un tailleur*.

To **take**	(something **from** somebody) *prendre (quelque chose à quelqu'un).* Ex.: *Je lui ai pris tout son argent,* I have taken all his money from him.
	(something to somebody) *porter (quelque chose à quelqu'un).*
	(somebody to a place) *conduire, mener (quelqu'un).*
To **take away**.	(to carry away) *emporter.* Ex.: Take that book away, *emportez ce livre.*
	(to lead away) *emmener.* Ex.: Take that child away, *emmenez cet enfant.*

Un **talon***	a heel.
Talons	*les serres (d'un oiseau de proie).*

To **tame**	(wild beasts) *dompter.*
	(birds, &c.) *apprivoiser.*

Une **tape***	a slap, a tap.
Some **tape**	*un ruban, une faveur.*

Taper*	to slap, to pat, to strike.
To **taper**	*s'effiler, se terminer en pointe*
A **taper**	(for churches) *un cierge.*

Un **tapis***	(*a*) a carpet.
	(*b*) a table-cover.

Une **targette*** . .	. a small bolt (on doors, &c.).
A **target** . .	. *une cible.*

Un **tas*** . .	. a heap.
Une **tasse*** . .	. a cup.

Tea . . .	. *du thé.*
Beef-tea . .	. *un bouillon, un consommé.*

Le **teint*** . .	. complexion.
La **teinte*** . .	. tint, hue.

Le **temps*** . . . (*a*) time.
(*b*) weather.
Quel temps fait-il? what sort of weather is it? what is the weather like?
Il fait beau temps, the weather is fine.
Dans le temps, formerly, of yore.
Avec le temps, in time, in the course of time.

Tendency . . . (notice the spelling) *une ten-d**ance**.*

Tenir* . . . to hold.
Tenez-vous là! stand there! stay there!
Tenez-vous en là, you had better be satisfied with that, you had better go no further in that matter.

Tenir à*	(followed by a verb) to be anxious. Ex.: *Il tient à savoir ce qui se passe,* he is anxious to know what is going on.
	(*quelque chose*) to value, to prize. Ex.: *Il tient à cette bague* (ring) *parce qu'elle appartenait à sa mère.*
	Il ne tient qu'à vous de..., it only depends upon you to...
Tenir de*	(*quelqu'un*) to resemble, to take after. Ex.: *Il tient de son père,* he takes after his father.
	Tenir une nouvelle de quelqu'un, to hear some news from somebody.

Un **terme***	(*a*) a quarter's rent.
	(*b*) end, termination. Ex.: *mettre un terme à...*, to put an end to...
Des **termes***	words.
Terms	(stipulated sum) *les conditions, le prix.*
A **term**	(three months) *un trimestre.*

Termination	(notice the spelling) *une terminaison.*

Terrace	(notice the spelling) *une terra*ss*e.*

Thick	*épais.*
	(turbid) *trouble.*

A tile	(on a roof) *une tuile*.
	(on a floor) *un carreau*.

Un **timbre***	(*a*) a bell (of an alarm clock, &c.).
	(*b*) a stamp (on paper).
	(*c*) a post-mark.
	Un timbre poste, a postage stamp.
	Le timbre de la voix, the tone of the voice.
Timber	*bois de charpente*.
	Timber tree, *arbre de haute futaie*.

Time	*le temps*.
	(when preceded by a number) *fois* (feminine). Ex.: I saw him three times, *Je l'ai vu trois fois*.
	(of day and night) *heure* (feminine). Ex.: What time is it? *Quelle heure est-il?*
	At times, *parfois*.
	Another time, *une autre fois*.
	The last time, *la dernière fois*.
	Once upon a time, *il y avait une fois*.
	Out of time (music), *à contretemps, pas en mesure*.
	Up to the present time, *jusqu'à présent*.
	To be behind one's time, *être en retard*.
	To be before one's time, *être en avance, être avant l'heure*.

In **time**	(in process of time) *avec le temps.* (in good season) *à temps.* Ex.: You come in time, *vous venez à temps.* (music) *en mesure.*
To keep **time**	(to be punctual) *être exact, être à l'heure, être ponctuel.* (of watches) *marcher bien, aller bien, aller à la minute.* (music) *aller en mesure.*

Timide*	bashful, shy.
Timid	*craintif, peureux.*

Tirer*	(*a*) to pull, to draw. (*b*) to shoot (fire-arms).
To **tire**	*fatiguer.*

Toile*	(*a*) linen, cloth. (*b*) drop scene (of a theatre). (*c*) canvas (for painting). *Toile cirée*, oil-cloth. *Toile d'araignée*, cobweb.
A **toil**	*un travail fatigant.*

The **top**	(of mountains, trees) *la cime.* (of a building) *le haut, le faîte.* (of the head) *le dessus, le sommet.* (of the water) *la surface.* (a plaything) *une toupie.*

Une **tortue***	(*a*) a tortoise. (*b*) a turtle.

Toujours*	(a) always.
	(b) still (adverb). Ex.: *Est-il toujours à Paris?* Is he still in Paris?
	(c) nevertheless. Ex.: *Toujours est-il que vous vous êtes trompé*, nevertheless, you deceived yourself; nevertheless, you made a mistake.

Un **tour***	(a) a turn.
	(b) a trick, a feat.
	(c) a lathe (a turner's machine).
	Tour à tour, by turns.
	A tour de rôle, in turn, in rotation.
	En un tour de main, in the twinkling of an eye.
Une **tour***	a tower.

Un **tourment***	a torment.
Une **tourmente***	a hurricane (at sea or on high mountains).

Tourner*	to turn.
Se **retourner***	(a) to turn oneself round.
	(b) to look behind.
Retourner à*	to go again to, to go back to.

Le **trafic***	trade, trading.
The **traffic**	*la circulation*.

Train* . . . train (railways).
Train direct, through train.
Train omnibus, slow train.
Train express, express train.
Train de marchandises, goods train.
Train de plaisir, excursion train.
Faire du train, to make a noise, a fuss.
Être en train de (familiar), to be in the act of doing something. Ex.: *Il est en train d'écrire*, he is writing.
Il nous a menés bon train, he drove us very fast.
Mener grand train, to live in grand style or to drive very fast.
A fond de train, at full speed.

Une **traîne*** . . train of a dress.

Un **trait*** . . . (*a*) an arrow, a dart.
(*b*) a trace (of harness).
(*c*) a feature.
(*d*) a dash (of the pen).
Tirer un trait, to draw a line (with a pen, &c.).
Avaler tout d'un trait, to swallow at one draught.
Un trait d'esprit, a witticism, a flash of wit.
Cheval de trait, a draught-horse.

Un **traitement*** . . (*a*) a treatment.
(*b*) salary, stipend, emoluments of a "*fonctionnaire*."

Un **traiteur***	an eating-house keeper.
A **traitor**	*un traître* (feminine, *une traîtresse*).

Le **trépas***	death (poetical word). *Les trépassés*, the dead.
Trespass	(jurisprudence) *violation de propriété*. (in Scripture) *une offense, un péché, une transgression*.

Trépasser*	to depart this life.
To **trespass**	(land, &c.) *violer la propriété de, entrer sans permission*. (to intrude) *abuser de*. (to sin) *pécher*. Trespassers will be prosecuted, *défense d'entrer sous peine d'amende*.

A **trial**	(an attempt) *un essai, une tentative*. (sorrow) *une épreuve*. (law) *un procès*.

Une **tribu***	a tribe.
Un **tribut***	a tribute.

Une **trique***	a cudgel.
A **trick**	(*a*) *un tour*. Ex.: To play any one a trick, *jouer un tour à quelqu'un*. (*b*) (of cards) *une levée*.

Trivial* . . .	vulgar. Ex.: *Une expression triviale*, a vulgar expression.
Trivial . . .	*insignifiant*.

Une **trombe*** . .	a waterspout (at sea).
Une **trompe*** .	trunk (of an elephant).

Un **trompette*** .	a trumpeter.
Une **trompette***	a trumpet.

Troubler* . . .	(*a*) to disconcert. Ex.: *La question de l'examinateur l'a troublé*, the examiner's question disconcerted him.
	(*b*) to make thick (beer, water, &c.).
	Troubler le repos public, to disturb the public peace.
	Sa vue se trouble, his sight is getting dim.
To **trouble** . .	(to disturb) *déranger*.
	(to distress) *chagriner, affliger*.
	(to vex) *ennuyer*.
	(a debtor) *importuner* (*un débiteur*).

Un **troupier***	(familiar) a soldier (infantry or cavalry).
A **trooper** . .	*un cavalier. Un soldat de cavalerie*.

Trouver*	(a) to find,
	(b) to like. Ex.: *Comment trouvez-vous son discours?* How do you like his speech?
	Trouver à redire à, to find fault with.
	Se trouver mal, to faint, or not to be comfortable.
	Vous trouverez bon que je sorte quand cela me plait, you will not object (ironical) to my going out when I choose.
To **try**	(to endeavour) *essayer*.
	(weights) *contrôler, vérifier, (des poids)*.
	(jurisprudence) *juger*.
	A tried friend, *un ami éprouvé*.
	To try a coat on, *essayer un habit*.
Un **tuteur***	(a) a guardian (of a child).
	(b) a prop (a support for plants and young trees).
A **tutor**	*un précepteur, un instituteur*.
A **tyrant**	(notice the spelling) *un tyran*.

U

Unison	(notice the spelling) *unisson*.
	In unison, *à l'unisson*.

To **use**	(to employ) *se servir de*.
	(to be in the habit of) *avoir l'habitude de, avoir la coutume de*.
User*	to wear out.
User de*.	to make use of.

A **utensil**	(notice the spelling) *un ustensile*.

V

Le **vague***	vacant space, vacancy. Ex.: *Regarder dans le vague*, to look at vacancy.
Une **vague***	a wave.

La **valeur***	(*a*) valour, bravery.
	(*b*) value, worth.

Valiant	(notice the spelling) *vaillant*.

Valable*	valid, available (tickets, &c.).
Valuable	*précieux*.

Un **van***	a winnowing fan.
A **van**	(a cart) *une charrette, un camion*.
Une **vanne***	a flood gate, sluice gate.

Vanter*	to praise, to extol.
Se **vanter***	to boast.
Venter*	to blow (of the wind).

Un **vapeur***.	a steamer.
La **vapeur***	vapour, steam.
	Une machine à vapeur, a steam-engine.

Un **vase***	a vase.
La **vase***	mire, slime.

Un **végétal***	(plur. *des végétaux*) plants in general.
Vegetables	*des légumes* (mas.).

La **veille***	(*a*) the day before. Ex.: *Je l'ai vu la veille de son départ.*
	(*b*) sitting up, watching (at night).
Une **vieille***	an old woman.
Une **vielle***	a hurdy-gurdy.
Une **veilleuse***.	a night-light, a float-light.

Venir*.	to come.
Venir à*	(*a*) to come to (a place).
	(*b*) to happen to. Ex.: *Si ma lettre venait à se perdre*, if my letter should happen to be lost.
Venir de*	(*a*) to come from (a place).
	(*b*) to have just. Ex.: *Il vient de partir*, he has just left.

Venomous	(of plants) *vénéneux*.
	(of animals) *venimeux*.

Le **vent*** . . .	the wind.
Une **vente*** . .	a sale.

Un **ver*** . . .	a worm.
Du **verre*** . .	some glass.
Un **verre*** . .	a tumbler, a glass.
Un **vers*** . .	a line (of poetry).
Vert* . .	green.

Une **verge*** . .	a rod.
Une **vergue*** .	a yard (to carry a sail).
The **verge** .	(the brink) *le bord*.
	(of a forest) *la lisière*.

Un **verger*** . .	an orchard.
A **verger** . .	(of a church) *un sacristain, un bedeau, un suisse*.

Une **veste*** . .	a jacket.
A **vest** . .	*un gilet*.

A **vice** . . .	(a fault) *un vice*.
	(a tool) *un étau*.
	Pauvreté n'est pas vice, poverty is no sin.
Une **vis*** . .	(pronounce **viss**) a screw (a kind of nail).

Viser* . . .	to aim.
Visser* . .	to screw.

La **voie***	road. *Une voie ferrée*, a railroad. *La voie lactée*, the Milky Way. *En venir aux voies de fait*, to come to blows.
La **voix***	(a) voice. (b) vote. Ex.: *Il a obtenu trois cents voix*. *De vive voix*, orally.
Un **voile***	a veil.
Une **voile***	a sail. *Mettre à la voile*, to set sail. *À pleines voiles*, with full sail.
Un **vol***	(a) a theft, a robbery. *Un vol de grand chemin*, a highway robbery. (b) flight (of birds).
Une **volée***	(a) a flight (of birds). (b) a volley (of guns). (c) a shower (of blows).
Un **volet***	a window shutter.
Voler*	(a) to fly. *Voler en éclats*, to fly into pieces. *Il ne l'a pas volé;* he richly deserves it, it serves him quite right. (b) to steal.
Volontaire*	(subs.) volunteer. (adj.) (a) wilful. (b) voluntary.
Volontairement*	voluntarily. Ex.: *Il est venu volontairement*, he came of his own free will.
Volontiers*	willingly, readily. Ex.: *Je le ferai volontiers*, I shall do it willingly.

W

Un **wagon***	a railway carriage, (also spelt *vagon*).
A **waggon**	*une charrette.* (military) *un fourgon.*
To **walk**	*marcher.* Ex.: *Il s'est fait mal à la jambe, il ne peut marcher*, he hurt his leg, he cannot walk. (for pleasure) *se promener (à pied).* To walk to a place, *aller à pied à.* To walk (so many miles) *faire (tant de kilomètres) à pied.* To walk up and down, *se promener en long et en large*, or *de long en large.*
To **water**	(plants) *arroser.* (animals) *donner à boire à, abreuver.*
West	(cardinal point) *l'ouest* (the "t" is sounded). (western countries) *l'occident.* My room faces the West, *ma chambre est au couchant.*
A **window**	(of a room) *une croisée, une fenêtre.* (of a shop) *une devanture.* (of a church) *un vitrail* (plur. *vitraux*).

Word	(one or several syllables written or spoken) *un mot.* Ex.: That word is badly written, *ce mot est mal écrit.* I could not hear the last word, *je n'ai pas pu entendre le dernier mot.* (speech) *des paroles.* Ex.: These words made a deep impression, *ces paroles firent une profonde impression.* (promise) *une parole.* Ex.: He has kept his word, *il a tenu parole* (or *sa parole*). He has broken his word, *il a manqué à sa parole.* Word of honour, *parole d'honneur.* In a word, *en un mot.* In other words, *en d'autres termes.* He answered in these words, *il répondit en ces termes.* Take my word for it, *croyez m'en.* I take you at your word, *je vous prends au mot.* A word to the wise is enough, *à bon entendeur, salut.*
Wrong	I am wrong, *j'ai tort.* This addition is wrong, *cette addition est fausse,* or *n'est pas juste, n'est pas exacte.* The wrong side of a cloth, *l'envers d'une étoffe.* The wrong side out, *à l'envers.* I have taken the wrong book, *je me suis trompé de livre,* or *je n'ai pas pris le livre qu'il fallait.* It is wrong of you to speak so, *c'est mal à vous,* or *c'est mal de votre part de parler ainsi.*

K 2

Y

A yard — (a court-yard) *une cour*.
(a poultry-yard) *une basse-cour*.
(a work-yard) *un chantier*.
(of a prison) *une cour, un préau*.
(a measure) about 91 "centimètres."
(navy) *une vergue*.

Yes — (*a*) *oui*.
(*b*) (in answer to a question in which there is a negative verb) *si*. Ex.: You did not understand?—Yes, I did. *Vous n'avez pas compris?—Si.* You do not know him?—Yes, I do. *Vous ne le connaissez pas?—Si.*

Yet — (already) *déjà*. Ex.: Has he arrived yet? *Est-il déjà arrivé?*
(with a negative) *encore*. Ex.: Not yet, *pas encore*.
(however) *cependant, pourtant, toutefois*. Ex.: Yet, you ought to know it, *cependant vous devriez le savoir*.

THE END.

THE
PUBLIC EXAMINATION
FRENCH HAND=BOOK

is divided into three parts :—

PART I (130 pages) contains 106 extracts from (chiefly) modern **FRENCH** authors for reading and translation.

PART II (130 pages) contains 132 extracts from (chiefly) modern **ENGLISH** authors for translation.

PART III contains questions on the **DICTIONARY OF DIFFICULTIES** met with in **FRENCH**.

N.B. — *The Public Examination French Hand-Book* is intended only for advanced pupils.

Second Edition.—4s. 6d.

The Companion work to Deshumbert's "Dictionary of Difficulties."

FRENCH IDIOMS AND PROVERBS

BY

DE V. PAYEN-PAYNE,

Univ. Lond. and France,
Assistant Master at King's College School, London.
Translator of the *"Memoirs of Bertrand Barère."*

Second Edition, Enlarged and Revised.

PRICE 2s. 6d.

Daily News.

"Gives in a concise form information valuable to students, which is only to be found scattered over the pages of large and expensive dictionaries."

Globe.

"Can be taken up at any moment and will always prove interesting and instructive at whatever page it is opened. The English equivalents of French idiomatic phrases are elegantly and correctly given in alphabetical order, explanatory notes being added when necessary."

University Correspondent.

"Quite the best book of its kind for the use of candidates for Military, Civil Service and University examinations."

Admiralty and Horse Guards Gazette.

"The special interest and value lie in the short notes discussing and explaining, as far as possible, the origin of difficult and obscure expressions."

Bookman.

"Compiled with great intelligence and real knowledge of the difficulties of English students of French."

Notes and Queries.

"Indispensable to all earnest students of the French language."

www.ingramcontent.com/pod-product-compliance
Lightning Source LLC
Chambersburg PA
CBHW031225170426
43191CB00031B/521